Geoffrey Robertson QC is one of the ... lawyers. He was appointed by the UN s ... as a distinguished jurist on the Internal J ... in many landmark cases, defending free speech and prosecuting tyrants and torturers such as Hastings Banda and General Pinochet. He has been credited with saving the lives of hundreds of prisoners through his arguments in the Privy Council against the death penalty, and with establishing vital free-speech rights in English law. His book *Crimes Against Humanity* has inspired the global justice movement: while *The Tyrannicide Brief* led to a re-evaluation of English Civil War history. His memoir, *The Justice Game*, has sold over 100,000 copies. He is a master of the Middle Temple, a visiting professor at London University and has served as president of the UN's War Crimes Court in Sierra Leone.

Robertson grew up in Sydney, where he qualified in law, subsequently taking up a Rhodes Scholarship. He returns regularly to conduct *Hypotheticals* and visit family with his wife, Kathy Lette, and their children.

The Statute of Liberty

How Australians Can Take Back Their Rights

Geoffrey Robertson

VINTAGE BOOKS
Australia

A Vintage book
Published by Random House Australia Pty Ltd
Level 3, 100 Pacific Highway, North Sydney NSW 2060
www.randomhouse.com.au

First published by Vintage in 2009

Addresses for companies within the Random House Group can be found at
www.randomhouse.com.au/offices

National Library of Australia
Cataloguing-in-Publication Entry

 Robertson, Geoffrey.
 The statute of liberty: how Australians can take back their rights.

 ISBN 978 1 74166 682 3 (pbk).

 Civil rights – Australia
 Human rights – Australia.
 Constitutional law – Australia – Interpretation and construction.

 342.94085

Cover design by Design by Committee
Typeset in 11/15pt Electra by Midland Typesetters, Australia
Printed and bound by Griffin Press

Random House Australia uses papers that are natural, renewable and recyclable
products and made from wood grown in sustainable forests. The logging and
manufacturing processes are expected to conform to the environmental
regulations of the country of origin.

Contents

'It is of great importance not only to guard society against the oppression of its rulers, but to guard one part of society against the injustice of the other part. If men were angels, no government would be necessary.'

James Madison, 1787

'In politics, if you see a head, you kick it.'

Hon. Douglas Anthony MHR, 1987

For my family

1

Over the Sea from Skye

The idea for this short book came to me on a snow-drizzled mountain on the Isle of Skye. I had been taken there by a television programme, *Who Do You Think You Are?*, to contemplate the poverty from which my peasant forbears had been rescued by the Reverend John Dunmore Lang.[1] In 1837 he persuaded the British government to ship poor but honest Highlanders from Scotland to Sydney, to save them from starvation and to counteract with their Calvinism the growing influence in the colony of the criminal Irish. They did not stay long in town but, homesick and hankering for the kind of mountain on which I stood, headed for the Eden-Monaro and became the men from Snowy River. One of their boys married into the family of an English squire, who had left his ancestral pile in Surrey in a hurry because he had made a maid pregnant. Unusually, for his time and class, he had married her, but to avoid the social shame he shipped off to Sydney, and in 1817 Governor Macquarie granted him all the land between Wollongong and Dapto (we've been everywhere, man . . .).

In due course the Robertsons came out of the bush and back to the big smoke – to the industrial suburb of Leich-hardt – where two of their teenage children, my great-uncles, volunteered for the First World War and were soon cut down in snipers' alley, Gallipoli. The next genera-tion was thrown out of work by the Depression and lost its favourite sons doing battle against Japan. On the front line in Townsville, my fighter-pilot father hit it off with the daughter of a Dapto school teacher, granddaughter of a mystery woman who had sailed in first class from Europe in 1848, the Year of Revolution. There is evidence, so the television researchers claimed, that she was of royal blood, fathered by Prince (later Kaiser) Wilhelm. At any event she was soon running the colony's first parliament in Sydney's Macquarie Street, looking after Sir Henry Parkes and the Reverend Dunmore Lang.

On that cold Scottish mountain, looking at sepia pictures of these early pioneers brought to Australia by hunger or by shame, and photos of the war-fallen soldiers and airmen, I wondered how to think of their struggles and their sacrifices. How should they be remembered, explained, celebrated, by those of us who are the fruits of their love and their labour? Do you simply lock away your history in a museum, or see it only on a granite monu-ment – 'For the fallen' – in a local park? Or can you make the struggles of your nation's past a vibrant part of your present and future, firstly by asking what values they were struggling for, and then by enshrining them in your culture and your communal behaviour – even, or particularly, in your law?

——

My own family story is typical of the stories of other fifth-generation Australians. I have managed to extend it a bit for my children's sake by marrying Kathy Lette, who comes from a long line of convicts (well, a forbear of hers came out in chains on the First Fleet).

By this stage – and this was the thought I extemporised on the mountain – we Australians had surely become a race. We don't think of ourselves as such: when the question is asked on an official form, we put 'Caucasian' or 'Asian' or 'Aboriginal', and we speak of 'Vietnamese Australians' and 'Lebanese Australians', as if one cannot shed ethnicity or an original nationality. This is a mistake, at least in terms of legal definition, where for the purposes of Race Relations Acts a 'race' is not defined eugenically or biologically, but by virtue of belonging to a distinctive group, which has built up common traits and beliefs through its history and inter-action over a lengthy period of time.[2] So by legal defini-tion we are all members of the Australian race, a distinctive grouping of people who have emerged from a geographical area with a unique culture, character and mindset.

In most progressive nations, 'Australians' are by law protected from discrimination and hate speech, though since it is one of our racial characteristics to sledge and be sledged, this is a protection we would probably wish to waive. For critical race theorists (who tell us that race is an historical and societal construct not necessarily related to biological difference) the truly defining character of a race is a sense of how its members' history has contributed to a distinctive moral outlook that they wish to preserve and to carry into their future.[3]

There are, lodged in our consciousness, various beliefs about 'the Australian way' of life, liberty and the pursuit of happiness, but they have not been synthesised or coherently articulated as a set of moral or legal values. We subscribe, of course, to UN treaties and to the Universal Declaration of Human Rights, but these are minimal standards (necessarily, because they are universal) and we have not improved upon them. We require new citizens to pledge their loyalty to a country and a people 'whose rights and liberties I respect', without defining these rights and liberties. We have given our children nothing they can recite with pride, except the doggerel in the national anthem, whose second verse we have a mental block about singing, for fear its words might encourage asylum seekers.[4]

This is regrettable for a nation that began its connection with the world as an open prison, and in due course made a 'fresh start' without the burden of expectations created by long social evolution or violent revolution.[5] Distance from the rest of the world has not been a tyranny, as Geoffrey Blainey would have it, but a real and increasing advantage: invasion and plague have not troubled us, we have acquired no special ideological fervour or savage class divisions, no view of ourselves as saints or missionaries ramming some 'ism' or other down foreigners' throats. We have inherited the best things about Britain – its institutions, its common law (however patchwork) and certain of its liberal traditions, including the Enlightenment preference for rationality over dogma. We have been joined, over two centuries, by people from Europe, America and Asia coming to Australia for refuge or profit or adventure, bringing us vivid memories of what they most valued in their culture, their family life and their traditions. We have taken a hard but yielding land, richer than most for primary industry and mineral wealth, and astonishing in its grave and shimmering beauty. We took it from an ancient and comparatively gentle people, who had occupied it for many thousands of years before the birth of Christ or the fall of Troy. If Australians have by now become a race, then Aborigines are included – they have taught the rest of us to dream, to be easygoing, to suffer adversity in silence and to find our way through the bush.

———

The Australian race – or to put our identity less controversially, the Australian people – emerged from a polyglot mixture of nationalities and other races: a kind of human minestrone. Not only a race, but a race apart, thanks to the kindness of distance. What distinctive moral vision have we attained from the struggles and sacrifices of our forbears? This is a question usually answered in generalities by politicians and prelates at services on Australia Day or Anzac Day, by academics in seminars on 'Australian studies' or by teachers at school assemblies. It is not normally perceived as a question that might be put to lawyers. But if our values are to be a living and working part of Australian lives – our entitlements, so to speak, from a pact with the state over the limits to which we should be subject to government power – then law must come into it. If we are to preserve that part of our heritage to do with freedom, we must write down clearly the entitlement of every citizen in the only way that politicians and public servants will understand and respect: that is, they must be written into law. If rights are not capable of legal enforcement then they are not rights at all. They are empty promises. A right must by definition be enforceable, which means it must be capable of assertion by lawyers and adjudicated by judges.

Although we talk today with some pride of the freedoms we enjoy and the liberties we value, and a government website tells new citizens that they have rights 'shared to some extent by all liberal democracies, adapted to Australia's unique setting', we have never taken the opportunity to set them down in writing in any covenant, by which those in power solemnly promise the people that they will not restrict them.[6]

Other advanced countries enshrine the rights for which their people have fought in a constitution. But when Australia came into existence as a political entity in 1901, the Australian race had not yet fully evolved. Its people were still essentially British in social complexion, loyalty and affinity. Legally, they even remained under British control – Australia's highest court sat in London, staffed by British judges – and its parliament was the 'imperial' parliament, in other words the British parliament, if it chose to govern by paramount force. Even the Australian constitution was a schedule to an imperial act. An attempt to insert into the constitution an important right to be fairly treated – a US-style 'due process' clause – was rejected for fear it might allow Chinese immigrants entry into the country. As for Aborigines, they were regarded as sub-human and hence could not be counted as citizens of the new nation.

Saying sorry to Indigenous Australians in 2008 proved something. It was a moment that engaged the nation's psyche across divisions of politics, religion and wealth. It had been preceded in 2006 by John Howard's history summit, which bemoaned our failing to teach or to interest students in our own history. Later, in April 2008, the new Labor government led by Kevin Rudd organised the Australia 2020 summit, at which a thousand articulate members of the community attempted to collect the best ideas for building a modern Australia. They came down in favour of a republic, a treaty and a charter of rights – three ideas that were new only in so far as they can be related to each other as essential conditions for the final emergence of an Australian identity. The republic is inevitable, and a more satisfactory settlement with Aboriginal Australians will undoubtedly be worked out. But the third element in this civic trifecta remains extraordinarily controversial.

Extraordinary to me, at any event, because in all the years I have worked with bills of rights in the UK and Europe and the Commonwealth, I have only ever found them a useful guarantee to citizens of what they can do without government interference. They provide, at a technical level, a modern and effective tool for courts to interpret legislation and to develop the common (in other words, judge-made) law in ways compatible with contemporary notions of fairness and human dignity. This means justice for people whose particular plight would never be noticed by parliament, or prove interesting enough to be raised by newspapers or by a constituency MP. Far from undermining democracy by shifting power to unelected judges, it shifts power back to unelected citizens: democracy from its inception has relied on judges ('unelected' precisely so they can be independent of party politics) to protect the rights of citizens against governments that abuse power. Indeed, there is now ample evidence from the UK showing that bills of rights improve democratic governance by making liberty a concern of politicians who would otherwise forget about it, and of public servants who might otherwise act arbitrarily or unfairly. As for the beneficiaries, they are all of us – children abused at school, old people who are not cared for properly, patients in hospitals, or vulnerable people suffering from mental illnesses. People who would otherwise be neglected and discriminated against, or treated with incivility by officialdom.

Of course, rights to human dignity may sometimes help a prisoner or an asylum seeker, but a true test of whether a society is civilised is whether it treats its most wretched members with a modicum of humanity. The most beneficial function of a charter of rights is to educate the people and to increase their awareness of the struggles and sacrifices that have produced the liberty it enshrines. There is a good deal of evidence from the US and Canada that such a charter strengthens both national identity and pride in liberal democracy.

On 10 December 2008, the sixtieth anniversary of the Universal Declaration of Human Rights, the Australian government established a national consultation into whether a charter – a statutory bill of rights – would work for Australia. There had already been much public debate. Commissions of enquiry in Victoria, Western Australia and Tasmania had studied the proposal closely and had reported that it would have positive results in their states, and the governments of the ACT and Victoria had already adopted a charter. But most Australian writing in favour of a bill of rights has come from lawyers, who do not find it easy to write for the general public, and the commission reports run to hundreds of pages and make for heavy reading.

The 'no' case, on the other hand, is presented in broad-brush slogans by clever wordsmiths who may not know what they are talking about, but who talk about it in popular newspapers in dramatic terms. They begin with a free kick: they argue that since many proponents are lawyers, they must be in it for the money. This image of fat-cat lawyers promoting a bill of rights to further their own greed is developed with great gusto by the ex-premier of New South Wales, Bob Carr, and by newspaper commentators and editorials in *The Australian*. In fact, the lawyers who generally take on human rights cases are employed in law centres or trade union offices or Aboriginal legal centres or universities, and they are paid much less than Macquarie Bank consultants or newspaper editors.

I must confess to being a proven lawyer, founder and head of the largest human rights chambers in Britain. I have spent much of my life arguing in courts around the world for men and women whose liberty is in peril from governments that abuse their power. As a result of many years' experience acting for victims of bad government in Britain and the Commonwealth, I became convinced of the importance of supplementing the common law with a bill of rights, and argued the case in Britain in *Freedom, the Individual and the Law*, published in 1993.[7] Five years later, a Human Rights Act was one of the first laws promulgated by the New Labour government. The prospect of returning to the fray to argue the case in Australia is not something I had expected: I have always considered my countrymen and women cautious but sensible in matters affecting their welfare and wellbeing, and had assumed that they would follow suit once the advantages of a statute of rights in a Westminster-style democracy became clear.

I reckoned without Bob Carr and John Howard and the bitter commentariat – the whinging comms – who deliver rights-bashing columns to the press. Whenever I return to Australia – several times a year – there is always an article written with edgy hysteria on the theme 'Beware, bad judges'. In 2008 we have had 'ACTIVIST JUDICIARY A LOOMING MENACE', 'POLLIES OR JUDGES TO RULE THE ROOST?', 'PUT THE BRAKES ON JUDICIAL HOONS', 'DON'T GIVE JUDGES ANY MORE POWER', 'MAD GAME TO TINKER WITH OUR GREAT SYSTEM', 'GIVING LAWYERS MORE POWER WILL CUT OUR LIBERTIES'.[8] These articles are full of misstatements of fact and misinterpretations of law. It may be that few read them, but I do not see why my fellow citizens should debate on the basis of mistaken facts or opinions that have little connection with reality. Of course they are answered, usually by the calm and correct Professors George Williams or Hilary Charlesworth, but their measured language lacks the excitement of articles about mad tyrant judges on the verge of seizing power.

When I began campaigning for a bill of rights for Britain, the argument against a bill was similar: in other words, 'Our liberties are safer in the hands of politicians than entrusted to unelected judges'. That is an absurd argument, because parliament does not deal in individual cases and is not equipped to remedy every – or any – particular case of ordinary citizens treated unfairly by the public service. It has no time to study or debate the thousands of individual grievances against public service bureaucracy decisions, or to work out the consequences to individuals of the thousands of pages of statutes that pass quickly through parliament each year, not to mention all the statutory instruments and regulations that are merely 'tabled' and are not read or debated. Moreover, a statutory bill of rights does not empower judges to overrule elected representatives, but merely to interpret their laws as consistently as possible with human rights. Under the procedure devised in the UK and copied in Victoria and the ACT, parliament remains sovereign. All a judge can do is issue a 'declaration of incompatibility', which invites parliament to look again at the statute. He or she cannot strike it down. The US Supreme Court regularly does that, in the greatest democracy in the world, where liberty has constitutional protection. In 2008, for example, it struck down a Bush law, which had been approved by Congress, denying habeas corpus – the right to be released unless the legality of your detention can be immediately established – to inmates of Camp Delta at Guantanamo Bay. But this power to strike down is a power that the people must vote, in a constitutional referendum, to entrust to the courts. A statutory bill of rights, or charter, does not empower judges to override laws made by elected representatives.

———

The Human Rights Act in Britain has brought many advantages. It has exposed numerous gaps in the common law – especially for disadvantaged groups. The main beneficiaries, however, have been ordinary citizens, given additional protection against unfair treatment. There has been no undermining of democratic governance. The separation of powers at the heart of any true democracy entrusts policy to parliament, and its fair and efficient implementation to a judiciary strictly independent of government. Nor has there been a flood of litigation – human rights arguments have actually replaced lengthier submissions based on endless old cases and precedents. The most important effect has been educational – teaching public servants how to protect human dignity when they deal with vulnerable people. Studies by the British Audit Commission and the Department of Constitutional Affairs have concluded that the act has encouraged 'new thinking' and has contributed to problem-solving in welfare services. It has not

been a 'get out of jail free' card for prisoners, although it
has improved their right to complain to journalists about
miscarriages of justice, and has ended the degrading
practice of 'slopping out' the excrement from their cells.
It has been effective most often in respect of homelessness, mental handicap, education, immigration, aged
care and disability services. In these cases, the areas that
should most gravely concern a prosperous and advanced
society, it has made a measurable contribution to good
government. There is some evidence that the first Australian
state charters (in the ACT and Victoria) are beginning to
have a similar effect.[9]

My main purpose in entering this debate in Australia,
however, is to expand it into a question of what kind
of society we were, we are, and we want to become. I
don't myself think it sufficient, although it may well be
convenient, to copy bills of rights adopted by other countries, or even by the United Nations. Granted, any statutory enumeration of basic freedoms should list those the
advanced world holds to be universal, but the statute
should be imbued with a spirit that reflects national pride
and national progress. In the United States, school children recite Thomas Jefferson's text from the Declaration
of Independence, a document that recalls the fervent
courage of men who risked bayoneting to defeat the
military might of King George III. In South Africa the
constitution reflects the rights – economic as well as social
rights – won after many years of struggle against apartheid. The adoption of a statutory charter would provide
an opportunity for Australians to incorporate some of their

struggles and achievements in the advance of human freedom, and to reflect traits that (optimistically perhaps) we regard as self-definitive.

By now, 221 years after British settlement of the continent, the Australian people have emerged as distinctive, not only in accent, character and geographical origin, but in beliefs forged over eight generations. Part of that distinctiveness is what can loosely be termed our heritage, including the stock of political rights and freedoms that forbears have battled or bargained for, and which have inspired our democratic institutions and ideals. Any charter we pass now should be infused with modern Australian standards: it should celebrate the best of our past as well as lessons from the worst; it should express our hopes for our future. It should be a guarantee to our children of the treatment they have a right to expect from government during their lifetime: not just the minimal treatment that governments everywhere are expected to afford their citizens, but standards that Australian governments proclaim to be inherent in Australian citizenship, drawn from the history and character of our people.

This book is not intended as a legal text, because a charter works for 'ordinary people' (a condescending phrase used by lawyers of persons who are not lawyers) and it is they who must understand it. I have tried to write simply about the law without becoming simplistic, although it will be necessary to use legal terminology to explain some cases from other countries, especially from Britain, that critics have misunderstood. One common theme in their negative writings is Australia's 'wonderful' record on human rights. I shall not spend much time refuting this proposition: we are way behind in protecting freedom of speech, while our recent policy of indefinite detention of asylum seekers and their children behind barbed wire at Woomera in South Australia disgusted the world. Neither dignity nor respect were accorded to Cornelia Rau or Vivian Alvarez Solon, or to David Hicks, abandoned for five years by his own government – unlike the British Guantanamo Bay prisoners, whose government did care about their human rights. Ministers and police alike ignored Dr Haneef's right to liberty, despite ASIO reporting him innocent. Saying sorry has not reduced the dreadful disproportion of young Aborigines in our prisons, or saved them from death on average seventeen years earlier than white Australians, or prevented higher rates of suicide in their youth than in any other country.

Many of those who argue against a bill of rights think we live in the best of all possible worlds, but they should think again. We may live in the best of all geographic locations, but the way we live – the life that we allow our poor, sick and vulnerable to live – is far from perfect. If the evidence shows that their lives can be measurably improved by a charter that draws on the best of our history and makes amends for the worst, surely we should embrace it.

—

The case for a statute of liberty – a charter, bill of rights, call it what you will – is set out firstly by examining how rights entered our history. By 'our' I mean British history – the common law that Captain Arthur Phillip brought to these shores with the First Fleet by raising the Union Jack at Sydney Cove in 1788. It is a proud history and many of our distant ancestors were part of it, but it was a work in progress. Then we see how it progressed, to the Universal Declaration, the 1998 Human Rights Act in the UK, and beyond to the most recent UN convention on the rights of the disabled. After that it's back to Australian history, to some of the achievements and struggles in building this country that might be defined and remembered today in the clauses of a charter. In the final chapter I provide a rough draft of the kind of statute of liberty that Australians might be willing to accept, as they contemplate President Barack Obama – a man who talks proudly of human rights because he is, in a sense, the creation of them, a beneficiary of the struggle for rights in the US, and of the Supreme Court decision in *Brown v. Board of Education*, which ended discrimination against blacks in education. Talk to him about the danger of unelected judges overriding Congress and you tell him to renounce his birthright.

I have spent my professional life making arguments based on bills of rights. Some have saved the lives of prisoners on death row, others have achieved release for dissidents wrongly detained by arrogant governments, or beaten up by over-powerful police.[10] Many of my clients have been journalists, and arguments based on free-speech guarantees have won them in Europe the right to protect their sources, to lift suppression orders and to publish responsible stories on matters of public importance without being successfully sued for defamation. I have invoked human rights on behalf of an Indian farmer in Fiji denied a right to democracy; on behalf of refugees in Hong Kong denied the right to join their families; on behalf of Catholics wrongfully detained in Singapore; and for victims of Zimbabwe's Robert Mugabe, Malawi's Hastings Banda and Chile's General Pinochet. I have used them on behalf of decent, law-abiding people who have been treated unfairly by government officials. I deployed them recently to stop a museum in Britain from experimenting on the remains of Tasmanian Aborigines, victims of a genocide once unleashed upon their people, and to force their return to Australia for burial. In none of these cases have unelected judges seized power from elected representatives – the Fiji case indeed restored democracy (all too briefly), and the others came to court because elected representatives declined to act, or were content that these issues should be decided by judges equipped by training and learning to make better decisions than parliament. That is all an Australian charter would do – but I believe it is enough, as I shall seek to demonstrate in the following pages, to make Australians of open mind and goodwill wish to adopt a statute of liberty.

2

The Rights of Humankind

uman rights are freedoms regarded as essential to the physical and mental wellbeing of individuals, allowing them a measure of dignity, imagination and self-respect. They empower us to make known our opinions, to mix with people of our choice, to protect the privacy of our home and family, and to be dealt with fairly, decently and lawfully by government. Some of these individual rights are absolute, such as the right to live free of torture or the right never to be held in slavery, but most are presumptive, in the sense that the law presumes individuals are entitled to a right, but in specific cases their claim may be overridden by considerations of the rights of others or of national security. Rights are sometimes divided into two categories: firstly, the civil and political, which can be directly asserted in the courts against governments and public servants who abuse their powers; and secondly, social and economic rights – to health care, education, housing and a clean environment. Many consider these to be 'aspirational' rather than legal, although some countries, most notably South Africa, have found ways to protect them in the courts.

Magna Carta is regarded as the first human rights charter. Clause 29 provides: 'To no man will we deny, to no man will we delay, justice or right.' It was, in its time – 1215 – little more than a squalid deal between King John and his barons, but it was refurbished by English parliamentary leaders in 1628 and became a central legal weapon in their struggle against the absolutist monarchy of Charles I. Magna Carta produced habeas corpus, 'the Great Writ', which allowed anyone detained by government officials to challenge the legality of their action in court. This right played a crucial role in the seventeenth-century struggles for supremacy between king and parliament.

Significantly, parliament's very first weapon in that battle was a bill of rights. Edward Coke, the chief justice sacked by the king after daring to suggest that judges should be independent, became an MP in 1628 and drafted the Declaration of Right, an updated version of Magna Carta, which parliament demanded that the king should treat as a legally binding statute. Charles I refused to regard it as anything more than a set of empty promises, and in 1629 he abolished parliament for eleven years. It is worth recording, for the benefit of those who claim that bills of rights are somehow anti-democratic, that they were in fact the first weapon used against tyranny by heroic MPs John Pym, John Hampden and Sir John Elliot, who risked their lives to establish the sovereignty of parliament.[1]

The English Civil War, in which parliament was victorious, was preceded by a battle over the independence of the judiciary. The king had ordered judges to deny habeas corpus to MPs he imprisoned, and directed them to decide the *Ship Money Case* in his favour by pretending that a tax he had imposed unlawfully – without parliamentary approval – was not a tax at all. The MPs who went to war for the rights of parliament knew that its long-term safeguard would be the independence of the judiciary and, for that very reason, one of the first things parliament did when it returned in 1640 and broke with the king was to pass a law changing the nature of judicial office. No longer could judges be sacked whenever they displeased the king, but only if they were guilty of serious misbehaviour.

So the men who first established parliamentary power knew something that politicians who rail against unelected judges do not: an independent judiciary, with power to interpret and develop the law, is an essential part of democracy. Later democratic theorists John Locke and Baron de Montesquieu explained that there must be a separation of powers between the legislature and the judiciary so the latter cannot be influenced in its task of applying parliament's statutes. Similarly, there must be a separation of power between the courts, on the one hand, and the executive government, i.e. ministers and the public service, on the other. This is crucial in cases affecting the liberty of the subject, if governments and their agents are to be called to account for wrongful or excessive abuse of the power that the people entrust them to use fairly and in the public interest.

The judiciary's independence is the first and most important bulwark of the liberty of the subject, because it will generally be the government that is bent on depriving the subject of liberty. If judges were required or pressured to decide cases in favour of government, there would be no bulwark at all. That is why parliament in 1641 abolished the court of Star Chamber, an 'executive' court of judges, bishops and crony politicians appointed by the king to torture and jail his critics (those who criticised the queen had their ears cut off and men suspected of treason, such as Guy Fawkes, were ordered to be stretched on the rack). Thus parliament, from its inception as a sovereign body, recognised that good government meant entrusting judges with the power to develop and apply the law, according to human rights rules of the time such as Magna Carta and habeas corpus.

That, at least, was the theory, and the theory of democratic governance is important. It has never meant that parliament can do anything it likes just because MPs happen to have been elected, or that governments can do anything because they are backed by a majority of elected MPs. Parliament in those days was not very democratic – MPs were elected only by men of property, and the case for universal male suffrage was not heard until Colonel Thomas Rainsborough raised his voice to Oliver Cromwell at the debate between the army and the Levellers at St Mary's Church in Putney in 1647: 'The poorest he that is in England has a life to live, as the greatest he; and therefore truly, Sir, I think it's clear that every man that is to live under a government ought first by his own consent to put himself under that government.'[2]

That famous debate, incidentally, endorsed a bill of rights drawn up by the Levellers, who made up the first political movement committed to egalitarian democracy. The Agreement of the People would have limited the power of parliament so it could pass no law restricting 'liberty of conscience in matters of religion' or introducing conscription. It provided that all laws must be 'no respecter of persons but apply equally to everyone: there must be no discrimination on grounds of tenure, estate, charter, degree, birth or place'.[3] Here, at the outset of the English radical tradition, we find that the earliest demands for democracy are qualified by guarantees that parliament will respect basic civic rights. It was also in this crucible period, when liberty was asserted against a tyrant king, that the rights (called 'privileges') of parliament were first established. When King Charles I arrived at Westminster with four hundred armed men to arrest Pym, Hampden and other leading MPs, the Speaker of the House famously defied him: 'I have neither eyes to see nor tongue to speak in this place, but as the House is pleased to direct me, whose servant I am here'.[4]

This is the basis of the constitutional convention that prevents the executive government – or the police or the army – from entering parliament without its permission. (In 2008 the Speaker of the UK's House of Commons forgot the convention and permitted police to search the office of an opposition MP to look for evidence that he had received leaked documents. It led to an almighty row, Conservatives and Labour alike demanding that this parliamentary privilege should be made more than merely a 'convention', by being included in a new and 'British' bill of rights.)

Come the Glorious Revolution in 1689, when parliament re-asserted its authority over the king but opted for a constitutional monarchy rather than a republic, a bill of rights again figured as one of its chosen constitutional devices. This bill remains important and may still be part of the law of Australia (nobody is very sure): it outlaws 'cruel and unusual punishments', excessive bail, and is the basis for absolute freedom of speech in parliament, hence the right of newspapers to report whatever MPs and senators say in parliament without being sued for defamation. It is a minor irony of the current debate that MPs who scoff at a bill of rights, or call it undemocratic, fail to recognise that they owe their parliamentary privilege of free speech precisely to the bill of rights of 1689.

Governor Phillip brought other important features of common law to the colony in 1788. Most notably, the right not to be a victim of torture, which the common law condemned – as one jurist put it, 'Torture is something that is done by the French.' It had occurred in Britain by Star Chamber warrants but after the Star Chamber was abolished, while all other European legal systems for several centuries required the torture of suspects, the British were protected by the common law from torture or other forcible means of self-incrimination. Indeed, the 'right to silence', another great principle of justice, was created by judges, not by parliament. The open justice principle, too – that the courts should always sit in public – was a rule developed by judges ('activist judges', as they would sneeringly be called by critics today). So was the right of jurors to bring back a verdict 'according to their conscience', against the wishes of the trial judge or the government, or even the evidence.

This great achievement came about in *Bushell's Case* in 1670, in which England's appeal judges granted habeas corpus to jurors who had been jailed by a furious trial judge for acquitting two Quakers, William Penn and William Mead, accused of holding an unlawful prayer meeting in the City of London.[5] The jurors had refused his direction to convict, even when forced to stay day and night in their jury room without food or fire or even a chamber pot. The court upheld the right of what historian E. P. Thompson later called 'the gang of twelve' to defy parliament's repressive laws, and bend or break the rules in order to deliver a 'sympathy verdict' according to their conscience. Jurors ever since have made significant use of this power to acquit those who have broken unpopular laws. In this respect, our liberties are in the keeping of unelected juries, entrusted with power to derail harsh criminal laws passed by parliament. The importance of that power for Australia, as we shall see, was that the country came into existence partly because of sympathy verdicts passed by juries who refused to be party to the hanging of thieves. Not only that, but demands from emancipists (freed convicts and their children) for the right to trial by jury was a key battleground in the process of building a free settlement from a penal colony.

For all the abuse that ignorant commentators hurl at

'activist judges', judicial activism has kept the common law up to date and, from time to time, nudged it to favour liberty. The First Fleet left an England whose citizens had been made secure against the government's trespass and intrusion on their property thanks to the judges who decided cases involving John Wilkes. Wilkes was a journalist and MP who assailed King George III, pointing out (quite correctly), 'You have never been acquainted with the language of truth until you heard it in the complaints of your subjects.' Government ministers authorised raids on his printers and his home, permitting anything to be seized (the treasury solicitor insisted that they take all his papers and even his stock of condoms). Wilkes sued and won massive damages on the basis that 'an Englishman's home is his castle', so that from then on no search warrants could be issued by government ministers (they had to go before a magistrate), and even properly issued warrants had to specify the nature of the material the police were allowed to seize.[6] This was the decision of a great activist judge Richard Pratt, and the mob that carried Wilkes in triumph from the courtroom knew exactly to whom credit was due: they chanted 'Pratt, Wilkes and liberty'. This signal victory for liberty was achieved not by parliament, cowed and corrupted by the king, but by a judge inspired by Magna Carta and the Declaration of Right.

The most dramatic development of human rights ideals came in 'that hour of universal ferment': the revolutions first of America (1775–83) and then of France (1788–91). Both were significant for Australia. Since the British could no longer dump convicts in America, their consequent prison overcrowding forced them to select Botany Bay as the alternative. The revolution in France and that nation's subsequent embroilment in European wars reduced its interest in the great south land and left this continent to be settled by the British – a pity, perhaps, for our style and cuisine, but a positive gain for self-government, cricket and the Church of England.

These revolutions against the tyranny of monarchs gave rise to stirring declarations about the rights of free men. The American declaration, drafted by Jefferson with help from Thomas Paine, identified the denial of human rights as justification for revolution: it promised fundamental rights to life, equality, liberty and the pursuit of happiness. But these were 'natural' rights, and were not drawn from any empirical source or discovered through rational argument. The proof of their God-given existence was simply that we feel and think we need them – they attach 'inalienably' to the human person, like a shadow. The French Declaration of the Rights of Man and the Citizen provided a detailed description of the 'natural, inalienable and sacred' rights that any French citizen could advance against an oppressive government. For all the blood shed to win them, these were not defined as 'human' rights, in the sense of universal values based on human dignity. They referred more to an act of faith than to a philosophy: as Alexander Hamilton, the legal architect of the American Constitution, put it, 'The sacred rights of mankind are not to be rummaged for amongst old parchments or musty records. They are written, as with a sun beam, in the whole volume of human nature by the hand of divinity itself, and can never be erased or obscured.'[7]

Nonetheless, in America they soon became legally enforceable, even against Congress, as the founding fathers intended. In the landmark case of *Marbury v. Madison* in 1803, the US Supreme Court explained:

> The very essence of civil liberties certainly consists in the right of every individual to claim the protection of the laws, whenever he receives an injury . . . the government of the United States has been emphatically termed a government of laws, and not of men. It will certainly cease to deserve this high appellation, if the laws furnish no remedy for the violation of a vested legal right.[8]

These legal rights were not only vested, they were honoured through the courage of those who had defied British sedition laws. American patriots revered John Wilkes (who supported their revolution at the time) and the memory of the Puritan leaders of 'the good old cause' (the English republic), such as Oliver Cromwell, the Levellers and the regicides, whose compatriots had founded New England. This explains (as Madison made clear to the Virginia Congress at the time) why the American constitution insists that government and parliament 'shall make no law' abridging freedom of speech, freedom of worship or the right to peaceful assembly. It explains why the Fourth Amendment secures people in their homes and persons 'against unreasonable searches and seizures', and the Fifth and Sixth enshrine 'due process', which gives rights against self-incrimination, double jeopardy and expropriation of property; rights to speedy, public and impartial trial with advanced disclosure of prosecution evidence; the right to cross-examine hostile witnesses and to call defence witnesses; and the right to counsel. Although protection from slavery was not added to the US constitution until 1865, America had in place by the beginning of the nineteenth century a functioning domestic court system in which basic human rights could be enforced, as such, by individual citizens.

The essential problem with the French and American declarations for the pragmatic and unemotional British was that they were based on the notion of 'natural' or God-given rights. This notion was powerfully debunked in 1794 by Jeremy Bentham as 'rhetorical nonsense – nonsence upon stilts', an argument he supported, ironically, by reference to the 'savages of New South Wales', who had no laws and therefore no rights – a common British misconception in the nineteenth century.[9] Then, predictably, such rights were attacked by Karl Marx, who called them bourgeois: 'Nothing but the rights of egotistical man . . . the right of selfishness.' In the nineteenth century, slavery was the only practice that came to incur general condemnation – outlawed first by Britain in 1807, but not by America until after its civil war. Nobody spoke of human rights, and indeed until shortly before the Second World War this concept was never used in political or intellectual discourse or at the League of Nations, even when Hitler began to extinguish civil liberties throughout Europe.

The revival of the notion of 'rights' deriving not from nature or God but from respect for human dignity owed much to H. G. Wells and a small group of English socialists – writers such as J. B. Priestly and A. A. Milne (who motored up from Pooh Corner to help with the drafting). As the war clouds gathered, they produced a Declaration of Rights for the 'parliamentary peoples' of the world. This was published in 1940 as a Penguin special, *H. G. Wells on the Rights of Man*.[10] It was translated into German by the War Ministry and dropped on SS divisions as they were overrunning France. The Nazis did not stop to read it, but President Franklin D. Roosevelt was inspired by the book to make his famous appeal in 1941 for 'a world formed on four essential freedoms – freedom of speech and worship, freedom from want and fear', On 1 January 1942, a few weeks after America's entry into the war, human rights became an official war aim. Australia joined with its allies to declare, in the Atlantic Charter, 'Complete victory over their enemies is essential . . . to preserve human rights and justice in their own lands as well as in other lands.'

This promise was furthered by the Nuremberg trials: its judgement on the major Nazi criminals, delivered on 30 September 1946, created an international criminal law under which individuals could be prosecuted for the most atrocious violations of human rights. Transcripts of the trial were delivered to Eleanor Roosevelt and her UN committee on which Australia was represented and in which it played a crucial part. As Australia's role in the foremost human rights treaty is rarely mentioned, it is worth examining in some detail.

—

The Universal Declaration of Human Rights is truly the 'Magna Carta of mankind', as Eleanor Roosevelt predicted on 10 December 1948 when she handed it to Dr Herbert Vere Evatt, president of the General Assembly of the United Nations, after a vote in which a few states abstained but none opposed. It was an iconic moment at the General Assembly's temporary headquarters at the Chaillot Palace in Paris, in the shadow of the Eiffel Tower; a moment that put Australia firmly on the diplomatic stage, not only because of 'Doc' Evatt's presidency (he was Australia's foreign minister at the time), but because of the remarkable part our tiny nation (whose population then was only seven million) had played in the eighty-one drafting sessions that had taken place behind closed doors over the preceding two years.

In that period the Australian delegation, instructed through Evatt's cablegrams from Canberra and led by the cantankerous Colonel Hodgson and the quick-witted Allan Watt, carved out a presence and position that at times confounded the Soviet Union, at other times defied the US and was often independent of Britain. In fact, in the endless to-ing and fro-ing that it took to hold the draft of the declaration together, as winds of the approaching Cold War threatened to tear it apart, the Australian delegation became crucial to the entire project because of the way it was able to win support from the unaligned but mildly socialist countries of Latin America, and eventually to build bridges with the Soviet Union.

It was not Gallipoli, actually, that first put Australia

on the international map – it was the conduct of Evatt and his team at the UN in this crucial period when the post-war human rights settlement was argued out and finally agreed, when our country had a genuinely independent foreign policy. Yet, today, diplomats Hodgson and Watt are rarely remembered, and the other Australians who feature in the record – Ralph Harry, A. J. D. Hood, E. J. R Heyward, G. A. Jockel, William McNamara – are names their country seems to have lost long ago. 'Doc' Evatt is recalled mainly for his unsuccessful leadership of Labor in his declining years, although it was his work as foreign minister that made him one of the most influential Australians of all time.[11]

Evatt made Australia's mark at the Paris Peace Conference in 1946, where he was the first to suggest the establishment of a European Court of Human Rights, which would have the power to admit individual complaints and make binding determinations for that ravaged continent. He argued that governments should not be trusted to protect the rights of individual citizens, as they could be ridden over roughshod by majorities prejudiced against them: 'State declarations, standing alone, are not sufficient to guarantee the inalienable rights of the individuals and behind them it is essential that some sufficient sanction be established.' Only a court could give legal remedies that would deter other states from abusing their powers. Evatt's vision, which came to pass in 1951, is the European Court of Human Rights at Strasbourg, and he is the true progenitor of the most influential human rights court in the world today.

Australia was elected to the UN's first Commission on Human Rights, and presented that body with a statute for an international court. To arguments from nervous delegations that such a court would impinge upon national sovereignty, the Australians feistily replied that sovereignty was 'an outmoded conception, a fetishest survival whose worship should be anathema in the face of economic and human inter-relationships of our one atomic world . . . gentlemen, every international agreement is a derogation of sovereignty!' Non-aligned countries were mightily impressed, and the UK and US were forced to concede the strength of the argument, although of course the Soviets opposed it from the outset and the Cold War made it unsustainable. It was later reversed by Robert Menzies and his foreign minister, Percy Spender, and Richard Casey, who opposed international cooperation in respect of human rights for fear it would come to target the White Australia policy and the treatment of Aborigines. But it is a remarkable fact – upon which Australians rarely remark – that Evatt and his delegates were first to beat the drum for policies that Amnesty International and other human rights organisations were to take up again in the 1990s, and which today are beginning to come to pass.

Australia's position from the outset was that the fifty-eight nations then making up the United Nations had a duty not only to agree on minimal universal values but to incorporate them in a convention that would bind all nations and have enforcement machinery based on an international court of human rights. Colonel Hodgson opened the first drafting session with a memorable challenge to Eleanor Roosevelt, who had left this difficult question off the agenda. He said, 'The commission should not confine itself to abstractions but was bound to consider immediately effective machinery for implementing human rights and fundamental freedoms in accordance with its solemn obligations.'

Australia was supported by France, Belgium and India, while Roosevelt wavered. The Australians, who were arguing for a convention to be implemented by a domestic statute in every country, which would require that country to accept the decisions of an international human rights court, were supported in a powerful submission by the American Bar Association. It was the Soviets, predictably, who sabotaged the Australian move, through the time-honoured delaying device of referring the matter to a sub-committee.

The Australians pressed on, pointing out that 'a mere declaration of principles would not offer assurance against the revival of oppression'. The US became more supportive and the British produced a draft convention: this time it was the French who blinked. 'The Australian proposal [for a court] would seem to be the normal step in the evolution of the world,' said René Cassin, later chairman of the UN Commission for Human Rights, 'but its realisation at this time seems unlikely.' Doubtless Monsieur Cassin at this point glanced over his shoulder at Stalin's hard men, whose boss, the Soviet foreign minister Andrey Vyshinsky, had been ringmaster of the Moscow show trials.

Having lost this argument through the hypocrisy of countries unprepared for any independent body to hold them to their pledges, Australia lobbied for a binding convention rather than a non-binding declaration. Here, initially, they had much more support, and only the Soviets objected that such a convention would be 'premature'. The weak-willed British were first to capitulate, and in due course the commission agreed to settle for a declaration. It is ironic to think that Australia, a nation that would subsequently shrink from adopting a statute of human rights, first earned its international spurs by its stance – widely respected at the time – in favour of a binding charter and an international human rights court.

Australia also played an important part in many of the debates over particular articles of the declaration. It called the bluff of the Soviet Union and its highly strung puppet states when they wanted to amend the right to 'independent and impartial' courts to 'open' courts (Stalin's rigged trials were always open but were never independent or impartial). It stood up for minorities: despite the reservations of the great powers (especially the US with its 'Jim Crow' segregation laws, and the Soviets with their subjugated peoples); Colonel Hodgson explained that human rights were all about protecting minorities from oppression, including the oppression of the majority in a democracy. Australia, with a fifty-year history of flourishing trade unions, was appalled to find these two words unmentioned in the first draft of the declaration, so they inserted them in Article 23.4: 'Everyone has the right to form and to join trade unions for the protection of his interests.'

Australia received applause from the Soviets and many other delegations when Allan Watt suggested the famous redrafting of Article 29.1. It originally read, ambiguously and, in either meaning, insipidly: 'Everyone has duties to the community which enables him fully to develop his personality.' Watt proposed a crucial change, to: 'Everyone has duties to the community in which *alone* [my italics] the full and free development of his personality is possible.' The insertion of 'alone' is striking, and it has been called the most important word in the whole declaration. It refutes the Marxist suggestion that human rights are merely those of egotistical man, of Crusoes (Robinson) with no ties to their community. It neatly makes the point that rights, being based on respect for human dignity, are necessarily mutual: the individual who is entitled to respect from his or her community must show respect to other members of the community if his or her entitlement is fully to be enjoyed, or is even worthy of being granted. This is why Article 29 goes on in sub-section 2 to subject individual rights to limitations that are prescribed by law for the purpose of securing recognition and respect for the rights and freedoms of others. Those who claim human rights do not acknowledge human responsibilities simply fail to understand Article 29.

—

Australia's greatest achievement was to ensure in the declaration the inclusion of social and economic rights. There had been concern about opposition from the US, and indeed about how such rights, for example to minimum standards of health and housing, would be enforced in the courts, especially against impoverished governments. Mrs Roosevelt's reluctance was overcome by the Australian delegation when Colonel Hodgson pointed out that her husband had famously declared the war was being fought for four freedoms, and the third was freedom from want. Mrs Roosevelt remarked that rights needed to be universal and not just 'for a progressive state like Australia', but she accepted that economic and social rights should at least feature in a declaration. Allan Watt assisted in the drafting of Article 22, which serves as the preamble to the economic, social and cultural rights:

> Everyone, as a member of society, has the right to social security and is entitled to realisation, through national effort and international cooperation and in accordance with the organisation and resources of each State, of the economic, social and cultural rights indispensable for his dignity and the free development of his personality.

Then follow the particular rights. To summarise, these are:

23. The right to work; to equal pay for equal work; to just remuneration; and the right to join trade unions.
24. The right to reasonable working hours and periodic holidays with pay.
25. The right to an adequate standard of living, including food, clothing, housing and medical care, and benefits in the event of unemployment, sickness, disability, widowhood or old age.
26. The right to free secular education, compulsory until secondary level, and to choose schools for your children.
27. The right to participate in cultural life.

The final version of the declaration has stood the test of time: sixty years on, it contains the language of modern liberty. There is anger flashing from its preamble. It recites as its rationale that since 'contempt for human rights have resulted in barbarous acts which have outraged the conscience of mankind', they should be protected by the rule of law. That, of course, meant they should be protected by law in every country. Although the drafters drew upon the eighteenth-century declarations, they wisely refrained from incorporating appeals to God or to nature. Instead they invoked the 'categorical imperative' familiar from the moral philosophy of Immanuel Kant: 'Act so that you treat humanity, whether in your own person or in that of another, always as an end and never as a means only.'[12] (I.e. 'Do unto others as you would have them do unto you.')Kant located the seat of universal laws in national respect for intrinsic human worthiness, which he termed 'dignity' – the key word in the preamble, which opens by recognising 'the inherent dignity . . . of all members of the human family' and goes on, by secular and rational argument, to affirm faith in 'the dignity and worth of the human person'.

What amazes today is the contemporaneity of the document. Eleanor Roosevelt's drafting committee produced an imperishable statement that has inspired more than two hundred international treaties, conventions and declarations, and the bills of rights found in many national constitutions that have been adopted since.

On 10 December 1948 she formally handed the Universal Declaration of Human Rights (UDHR), to Dr Evatt, who announced the advent of a new international law of human rights. He said, 'Millions of men, women and children, all over the world, will turn for help, guidance and inspiration to this document.' This declaration is the centrepiece of the human rights triptych, which had begun the previous day by unveiling the Convention against Genocide, and was completed in March 1949 by the Geneva Conventions on the treatment of prisoners of war and the protection of civilians during war. The Universal Declaration was proclaimed by the General Assembly as 'a common standard of achievement for all peoples and all nations', to be promoted by education and in particular by 'progressive measures, national and international, to secure their universal and effective recognition and observance'.

Australia, unlike all other progressive members, has taken no national measures to secure the effective recognition of these universal rights by passing them into its law – in other words, by legislating a bill of rights.

———

Although the Universal Declaration is not enforceable as such (it is a declaration, not a convention or a treaty, which states have bound themselves to enforce) it has become the human rights bedrock and is regularly quoted by courts, textbooks and NGOs as setting the standard for the way in which all states must treat their citizens. The provisions of the declaration are now further elaborated in the International Covenant on Civil and Political Rights (ICCPR) and the International Covenant on Economic, Social and Cultural Rights (ICESCR), which both came into force in 1976 and have since been ratified by a large majority of countries. Although these have no enforcement provisions, the ICCPR does have a tribunal (the Human Rights Committee) which issues opinions on complaints by individuals whose states are prepared to subject themselves to its criticism. Australia has had fourteen complaints upheld (the third-largest number for any state) and was obliged to require Tasmania to repeal its laws against homosexuality as a result of one case brought to this committee.

There are regional human rights treaties covering Latin America (overviewed by the Inter-American Court of Human Rights) and Africa, which has no court as yet, but merely a poorly drafted convention ignored by African rulers. The most effective system is the one suggested by Evatt in 1946 – the European Court of Human Rights, which sits in Strasbourg and decides whether the laws and court decisions of the forty-seven member states of the Council of Europe have breached the European Convention of Human Rights. (The Council of Europe was founded in 1949 to develop democratic principles within Europe.) If a member state is found in breach it is effectively bound, within six months of the decision, to revise its offending law to bring it into conformity with the convention.

There are a number of conventions dealing with specific human rights concerns – against torture, apartheid and racial discrimination, for example – and endorsing the rights of women, children and persons subject to disabilities. These are not directly enforceable, unless a breach is so serious that it amounts to a 'crime against humanity' – namely murder, torture, enslavement or severe imprisonment – if committed as part of a widespread and systematic attack on a civilian population. These international crimes, together with war crimes, are defined in the 1998 Treaty of Rome, which established the International Criminal Court. Violations that are not of this severity are left to domestic law enforcement. The extent and quality of the protection of human rights by a nation are subject to scrutiny every few years at the UN's Human Rights Council, where NGOs such as Amnesty International and Human Rights Watch will be able to comment on its performance. This is not, however, an occasion for more than diplomatic finger-wagging: the council has no power other than publicity. Australia has been criticised recently, especially for its indefinite detention of asylum seekers and for its treatment of its Indigenous people.

The universality of human rights has been challenged in a number of respects. It has been alleged by some Asian states that the concept reflects Western values, which are individualistic rather than community-based. These criticisms, usually made by political leaders who persecute opponents and jail or torture critics, are self-serving and ignore the fact that rights as formulated in the Universal Declaration are not so much fundamental as elemental, and are subject (except in cases of the right to be free from slavery or torture) to qualifications necessary in democratic society to protect social interests such as public order, national security and the rights and freedoms of others.

A more dramatic challenge has been posed by the so-called War on Terror, which has been said to justify, for example, the ill-treatment of suspects and their permanent detention without trial. The worldwide condemnation heaped on the US over its use of torture techniques such as waterboarding, and its denial of habeas corpus and fair trial at Guantanamo Bay, shows how counter-productive it can be to disregard human rights. Note, too, how the photographs of prisoner torture at Abu Ghraib prison became recruiting posters for al-Qaeda, alienating communities whose support is needed if terrorists are to be isolated and unmasked.[13]

Enforcement of human rights standards in Britain has been revolutionised by the Human Rights Act of 1998, which made the European Convention enforceable in the British courts. Although the common law and ensuing legislation incorporated Magna Carta and firmly protected habeas corpus, open justice and free trial, it was deficient in its support for free speech and its opposition to discrimination, and offered little protection to privacy. These, and other gaps in legislation have now been covered, and courts have the power, as far as it is possible, to interpret laws so they are consistent with human rights standards.

There is still a lot of loose talk about 'rights' and associated concepts – 'duties', 'responsibilities', 'freedoms' and so on. I take the positivist position that a 'right' does not really exist unless it is capable of enforcement. That means you should be able to go to a court and obtain an order to stop the government or its agencies abusing their powers, whether by police holding you unlawfully in the cells, or the state seizing your property without paying compensation, or the education department refusing to school your child with learning difficulties, or just some bloody-minded bureaucrat treating you unfairly. If you have a right, then you have an entitlement to a court order that will force the government to stop such abuse, pay your court costs and in some cases, where you have suffered real damage, pay you compensation. But it takes a law – a bill of rights in the form of a statute – to provide the court with that power. Judges have some power to protect liberty, by interpreting existing laws (statutes) passed by parliament and by developing the common law (the body of law parliament leaves to judges to develop through decided cases). But, thanks to the remarkable capacity for ambiguity in the English language – a capacity humorously exploited through puns and *doubles entendres* by writers from Shakespeare to Lette – and to the often limited ability or imagination of parliamentary draftsmen, statutes are very often capable of different interpretations – some consistent with rights, and some not.

Anglo-Australian common law, which comprises decided cases (some centuries old), has many gaps and omissions. Since it was made originally by British judges, it takes little account of rights of free speech, or privacy, or environmental protection. It can be developed – but not always consistently with liberty, unless there is a rule that it should be developed in that direction. This rule – that judges must interpret and develop the law in a way that is consistent with a wish for as much liberty as a democratic society can reasonably bestow – is supplied, in all advanced democracies except Australia, by a bill of rights.

———

There is, at the outset, an important distinction to be made between a constitutional bill of rights and a statutory bill of rights. For historical reasons, certain countries – notably the United States after its bloody war of independence against George III; Germany when it picked up the pieces left by Hitler's tyranny; and South Africa when it emerged, led by Nelson Mandela, from the dark days of apartheid – chose to entrench the liberties for which they had fought in new constitutions. These give the highest courts, such as the US Supreme Court and the South African and German constitutional courts, the power to strike down laws passed by parliament. Is this undemocratic? Of course not – the suggestion is absurd (although, as we shall see, it is made by most Australian opponents of a bill of rights). As Professor Ronald Dworkin, the leading juristic philosopher, explains:

> The single triumph of democracy in our time is the growing acceptance and enforcement of a crucial idea: that democracy is not the same thing as majority rule, and that in a real democracy liberty and minorities have legal protection in the form of a written constitution that even parliament cannot

change to suit its whim or policy. Under that vision of democracy, a bill of individual constitutional rights is part of fundamental law, and judges, who are not elected and who are therefore removed from the pressures of partisan politics, are responsible for interpreting and enforcing that bill of rights as they are for all other parts of the legal system.[14]

There can be no suggestion that the US is undemocratic because it entrusts judges with the power to overrule its elected Congress in order to protect the liberties of its citizens – liberties that its founding fathers in their wisdom insisted should not be left to the mercy of Congressional majorities or presidential figures like George W. Bush or Sarah Palin. These men believed that certain rights that protect life, liberty and the pursuit of happiness were inalienable, and that true democracy means entrusting a bench of nine judges with the authority to strike down any law that breached these rights, no matter whether it had unanimous support in Congress and from the president (in other words from the legislative and executive branches of government).

Thus, in 2008, the liberty of the most wretched on Earth – the prisoners at Guantanamo Bay – was protected by the Supreme Court, who decided that the Bush administration law passed by Congress to abolish habeas corpus for 'enemy combatants' was unconstitutional. This was the end of that attack on liberty – Congress could not defy the Supreme Court or pass another law to get round its ruling.

Americans have the purest form of democracy, and those bred in the Australian (read, the British) system wonder at it. The notion of electing judges sounds horrific to their ears – complaints abound that it politicises appointments to the bench. Yet in practice, in those American states where judges are elected, they are nominated by political parties who usually put up good, experienced candidates. And at the US Supreme Court level bad candidates such as Harrold Carswell (a racist), Harriet Miers (an incompetent) and Robert Bork (an ideologue) can be rejected, if need be after thorough invigilation by an all-party Senate Committee. The result is a level of democratic debate over legal appointments that Australian opponents (and supporters) of a charter are too frightened to contemplate. The Rudd government has expressly excluded advocates of the US system from its national consultation. Yet the secretive and undemocratic Australian system allows a prime minister to appoint an ideological crony to the High Court bench without the slightest public scrutiny from our supine Senate. Despite complaints about 'unelected judges' it is never suggested in Australia that we should elect them, or that we should devise a system where High Court judges would be appointed on merit, after an open competition, rather than being chosen (often for partisan reasons) by the prime minister.

Political meddling in the appointment of Australian judges is one of the most unsatisfactory aspects of our legal system.[15] Under the influence of a bill of rights in Britain, with its guarantee of an independent judiciary, appointments to the higher courts have been taken out of the hands of politicians and given over to expert selection committees, which advertise the positions and invigilate the candidates. For UN judges, the Internal Justice Council, on which I sit, not only advertises the positions but actually subjects candidates to a three-hour written examination – a sure way, I can attest, of finding out true judicial merit (and eliminating those lazy judges who have their associates write their decisions).

The pros and cons of the American system are endlessly arguable, but not in this book: it is not the model that is advocated here, and it is described only to avoid the confusion that bogs down discussions in this country about bills of rights. My model – that of the ACT, Victoria and the UK – is statutory and not constitutional, and hence would not allow judges to strike down laws passed by parliament. There is, of course, nothing undemocratic – as Dworkin explains – about entrusting the courts with that power. Britain and all forty-seven countries that belong to the Council of Europe have done that indirectly, by allowing the European Court of Human Rights at Strasbourg to declare any of their laws a breach of the European Convention, in which case they are bound by treaty to repeal or alter that law within six months of the decision. There are further examples, provided by many of the countries we play cricket with. They received their 'independence' constitutions from Britain in the 1960s with a constitutional bill of rights, under which their courts could strike down parliamentary laws that were in breach of fundamental freedoms, subject to the final decision of the top judges in London – the law lords, sitting as the Privy Council. Jamaica and Trinidad, Barbados and Mauritius are all in this category: several have now adopted new republican constitutions, but none have repealed the bill of rights provisions or wished to stop the Privy Council – which is now, in effect, their external human rights court – from safeguarding their citizens against oppressive government, lazy parliaments or unfair public servants.

—

What is the alternative to constitutional protection of liberty? Some commentators in Australia think there should be no protection at all. Parliament, they argue, must have unlimited legal power to do everything and anything it wishes. If it passes a law to cut out the tongues of citizens with red hair, then so be it – if there is nothing in the Australian constitution to stop them (and there is not) let the voices of citizens with red hair be heard no more in the land. Parliament, they say, should have the power to do nothing at all if it wishes – and MPs attend so irregularly, and at such short sessions, that there is a lot they do not do. This notion, that parliament should be entirely unhindered in doing anything it likes, or not doing everything that is necessary, is popular with some pundits, who hail it as democratic, although, as we have seen, the modern founders of the democratic ideal have never regarded it as such.

There is a halfway house between constitutional protection of liberty and no protection at all. This is found in a statutory bill of rights: legislation directing the courts, where a statute is ambiguous or the common law unclear, to interpret and develop law consistently, so far as possible, with human rights principles. Even if a law is obviously in breach of these principles, the courts cannot abolish it or strike it down: they issue instead a 'declaration of incompatibility', which draws the inconsistency to parliament's attention. Even then, parliament does not have to do anything, although it may decide to amend or re-write the offending law rather than to leave it as it is.

There is no conceivable threat to democracy in having a statutory bill of rights of this kind. In 2004 the ACT adopted one – the first in Australia – and in 2006 Victoria became the first Australian state to enact a bill of rights. There the skies have not fallen. On the contrary, there is evidence (and it is early days) of improvements in parliament's consideration of human rights questions, because they are more often identified and debated, with more informed and intelligent argument. Commissions of enquiry in Tasmania and Western Australia in 2007 also advocated a charter of rights for their states.

There is a terminological confusion about Human Rights Acts, incidentally. These statutory bills of rights, as they are called in Britain, tend to be referred to as 'charters' in Australia. (In Britain, a 'charter' denotes a voluntary agreement to respect rights and is not highly regarded: 'citizens' charters' proved worthless because they were unenforceable.) Hereafter I shall use 'charter', 'statutory bill of rights' and 'liberty bill' interchangeably, while begging the reader not to confuse them with bills of rights enshrined in constitutions. Of course, the statute may lead to the constitution:

that happened in Canada, where a non-binding statutory bill passed by parliament in 1960 was, in 1982, under Pierre Trudeau's lead, adopted by the peoples' representatives to become part of their constitution.

The Canadian example is interesting because it shows how a statute that initially may only have been passed as a result of support of the governing party can, over time, capture the public imagination and be upgraded by popular demand into an all-powerful constitutional provision. This provides a good reason for Australia to begin with a statute, enabling some experience of its working before the public is asked to entrench it in our constitution.

The language of most charters uses definitions found in international instruments: the Universal Declaration of Human Rights, the ICCPR, and the European Convention on Human Rights. The latter document, because of the respect accorded to it at its court at Strasbourg, provides the most extensive jurisprudence on what defines a human rights breach. Although drafted by British lawyers in 1950, the European Convention is Eurocentric (there is no right to jury trial, for example, because Napoleon abolished juries throughout Europe) and it lacks reference to recent human rights developments such as the UN Convention on the Rights of Persons with Disabilities, which only came into force in 2008.

There are now demands in the UK for a more up-to-date 'British bill of rights' than the 1951 European Convention, and focused on the nation's unique contributions to liberty. That approach should be adopted for an Australian charter. Some rights mean a lot to us because they reflect iconic moments in our history. These include lowlights as well as highlights of our national caravanserai: idealistic moments of moral vision (for example, Phillip's first law against slavery, the emancipist fight for trial by jury, press freedom, later advances in securing free education and universal suffrage) and events to which we must say 'never again', such as the massacres at Myall Creek, Risdon Cove and Lambing Flat, and the killings at the Eureka Stockade. We need a statute of liberty with a preamble that children can learn at school and recite with pride; one that will reflect the unique history that has influenced our definition of a free society. And if we need a bill of rights for modern, practical purposes – and I shall argue that we do – then these symbolic moments should be reflected in its language.

3

So-called 'Rights' of Australians

Australia's very first law is now regarded as the most fundamental of human rights. It was written in 1787 by Captain Arthur Phillip, waiting while the First Fleet was, at his humane insistence, being fully provisioned for its eight-month voyage. 'There can be no slavery in a free land,' he decreed, 'and consequently no slaves.' At this time, many of America's more celebrated founding fathers were whipping, selling or impregnating their slaves; it would be twenty years before Britain passed a law against slavery, and fully a century before other leading nations, at the 1878 Congress of Berlin, forswore this evil trade in human flesh. Are Australians proud of Phillip's landmark law? Most have not heard of it. It is not mentioned in our classrooms and has never been noticed by any judge in any court in the country. So much for the pride we have in the potentially iconic moments of our history – they are there for the taking, yet we fail to celebrate them or make them any part of our civic life.

In this chapter I want to observe, as if from space, the relationship in Australia between government and citizen: what rights people have and how they fit into the constitutional framework. It is odd, to say the least, that the state has always been headed by a foreigner, via an arrangement that discriminates on grounds of race, sex and religion. The explanation is found in the fact that Australia was assembled by men who were British in loyalty and racist (by today's standards) in outlook: they regarded 'rights' over and above those granted by common law as unnecessary and probably dangerous. In consequence there is a systemic defect in our constitutional arrangements, a yawning gap that might be closed – or at least narrowed – by a statute of liberty.

How many Australians know the year in which their nation became independent? To this elementary question there are seven arguable answers:

• The year of Federation, 1901
But this was an act of the British parliament, which could have repealed Australia the very next day, since it could still impose its legislation. Australian law was still under the control of British judges sitting in the Privy Council. Every state parliament remained subject to the British Crown. The governor-general of Australia was to be appointed directly by the British government, without consultation with the Australian government, and state

governors were appointed on the advice of the British Colonial Office, not of the state premier.

• The Statute of Westminster, 1931
This was an act of the British parliament, sitting as parliament for the dominions, and adopting a resolution from an imperial conference in 1926 (the Balfour Declaration), which permitted the federal parliament to amend or repeal British legislation applying to Australia, but did not give state parliaments this power. The common-law rule giving supremacy to British statutes still applied; Australia's final court of appeal remained the British law lords sitting in the Privy Council in London. In any event, Australia did not adopt the statute until 1942, although in 1931 the Australian government was finally and graciously allowed to advise the monarch about whom he (in other words, the British government) should appoint as governor-general, though not as state governors.

• The Statute of Westminster Adoption Act, 1939
This was passed in 1942, but it was backdated to 3 September 1939, which thus becomes a possible date for Australian independence. But on this very day the Australian government believed itself legally bound by the British declaration of war on Germany, as Robert Menzies QC, its then prime minister, made clear. Since the power to declare war is fundamental to an independent nation, Australia did not have independence.

• Declaration of war on Japan, 1941

The Curtin government acted on its own initiative to declare this war. But the legal bonds to Britain remained, notwithstanding the fall of Singapore.

• The Statute of Westminster Adoption Act, 1942

This was passed by the Australian parliament to remove doubts about the validity of Australian laws that might previously have been struck down as repugnant to British law, and to remove the right of the British parliament to pass laws affecting Australia, other than at the request of the federal government. This did not apply to the states and did not remove the Privy Council as our final court of appeal. The Adoption Act was passed in October 1942, but was made retrospective to 3 September 1939, when Britain took Australia to war.

• The Australia Acts, 1986

Seven laws enacted by the states, the British government and finally by the Commonwealth government severed the constitutional tie to Britain, but the British monarch remained head of Australia. No longer could the queen exercise her powers on the advice of the British Foreign and Commonwealth Office rather than the state governments, and the power of the British parliament to legislate for Australia was finally abolished. With it went the absurdity of having Australia's highest court manned by British law lords, who were often intellectually inferior to our High Court judges and out of touch with the nation whose legal disputes they were deciding from their chamber in Downing Street. The British monarch remained untouched as Australia's head of state.

• Not Yet

An obscure seventeenth-century German princess, Sophia of Hanover, has had her genes enshrined in the Australian constitution's pride of place. Those of Princess Sophia's descendants who mount the British throne automatically become head of state in Australia. The constitution remains part of a British law – the British parliament's Common-wealth of Australia Constitution Act 1900 (the orig-inal is lodged in a public records office in London), although the source of federal power is now the Australian constitution, which can be by section 128 amended or replaced by the Australian people voting in a referendum. So the source of federal power in Australia remains the UK parliament, until Australia decides to adopt a new constitution.

Australia is one of the few nations that lacks an 'independence day'. This is a day of pride in other countries, but is here a matter of indifference other than to constitutional lawyers, to whom it is a matter of confusion. No doubt to our grandchildren it will be a matter of curiosity that for so long one our most important public offices – the Australian head of state – was closed to all except members of one massively privileged family, hailing from another country.

The 1701 Act of Settlement, which defines the UK (and hence the Australian) crown, is a blood-curdling anti-Catholic rant, which provides that any monarch who holds communion with the Church of Rome or marries a papist – heaven forbid a Hindu or Methodist or Rastafarian – must be immediately dethroned. This primitive British law enshrines religious intolerance in the very bedrock of our constitution. Its rules of royal succession are based on the feudal principle of primogeniture: inheritance down the male line, in blatant contravention of our Sex Discrimination Act. If Prince Charles converted to Catholicism or had a sex-change operation, the crown would go to his male children, then to his male brothers ahead of their older female sister. But why should the office of head of Australia go to any of these members of a white Anglo-German Protestant dynasty, winners some centuries ago of 'Britain's top model family' competition?

We have been through this before, you might think, during the 1999 referendum. But we haven't. Then, the main argument of the 'yes' republicans was the need to have an Australian as head of state. This argument has never seemed definitive: we could do quite well by electing Rupert Murdoch (an American), Richard Branson, Nelson Mandela or Angelina Jolie as our head. What is objectionable about our present arrangements is that a constituent part of our parliament, 'which shall consist of the Queen, the Senate and the House of Representatives' (Section 1) is a monarch, and the monarch of another country. She has the power to defeat democracy (because 'the Queen may disallow any law within one year'); delay it ('A proposed law reserved for the Queen's pleasure shall not have any force'); direct its operation ('The executive power of the Commonwealth is vested in the Queen'); and by her power of appointment controls its armed forces ('The Commander in Chief of the naval military forces of the Commonwealth is vested in the Governor-General as the Queen's representative').[1] Our head of state is defined by a law that is sexist, racist, anti-meritocratic and discriminatory on grounds of religion. Thomas Paine's famous point, that an hereditary monarch is as absurd as an hereditary poet or an hereditary mathematician, may fail to take account of the entertainment value provided by the lesser royals, although their antics would doubtless still feature in our tabloids long after the heir-conditioning had been removed from our constitution.

Australia entered the twenty-first century lacking the symbols of independent statehood: it does not have a democratically elected head of state, it does not have any compact with its original inhabitants, and it does not articulate the rights of its citizens. Why not?

—

At Federation, the founding fathers agreed with the British government to put to the vote (a vote from which women, blacks and Territorians were excluded) a constitution that said little about human rights – understandably, because at this time they did not exist as a legal concept. Besides, Britain did not need to leave a bill of rights in place to protect the people from irresponsible government: Australian statesmen, avowedly British to their bootstraps (or, as old photos show, from their bowler hats to their brogue shoes) had willingly agreed that Australian common law would remain British common law; that the British law lords would oversee, and overrule, the Australian courts. British law and British judges sitting in Australia's final appeal court in the Privy Council in Downing Street were essential, the Colonial Office explained, for British investments. Investors would feel secure if friendly law lords in London could decide any claim against an Australian. This was the main condition imposed by the mother country, a mother that had to push its reluctant young out of the nest. Earl Grey, the colonial secretary, had greatly upset nervous Australians as early as 1850 by suggesting they federate. In 1890 the Colonial Office began to worry about French and German settlement in the Pacific, and was even more determined for Australian states to grow up and federate, and develop a national defence capacity.

Federation came not from a struggle against Britain, which urged it on, but from the struggle by Sir Henry Parkes – the father of Federation – to convince Australians in different states that there was a 'crimson thread of kinship' running through them all. Embarrassingly for the next-of-kin today, the crimson thread that united them by 1900 was not a belief in human dignity, but a fervent desire for racial purity. The national objects of Federation were to enable a common defence policy, the abolition of interstate customs duties, a national currency and postal service, and so on, but it drew its main emotional support from a desire to erect a barrier against Chinese immigration and to stop Queensland planters importing Kanakas from the Pacific Islands. The trade unions had some justification for wanting limits to an influx of cheap labour, although this was usually expressed in racist terms and much of the rhetoric from the middle classes was about the evils of miscegenation. An attempt at the 1898 Melbourne Constitutional Convention to inject into the draft of the Australian constitution the great US guarantees of equality and due process was rejected after Isaac Isaacs (much later the first Australian governor-general) warned of the 'danger' of ending racial discrimination against Chinese workers, and Sir John Forrest, premier of Western Australia, openly spoke of the 'great feeling' Australians had against 'coloured peoples'. He had just passed a law, which other states would copy, that 'no Asiatic or African alien can get a miner's right or go mining on a goldfield' and he did not want it challenged. Henry Higgins, later a High Court judge, assured Sir John that by rejecting the US equal rights clause he could ban Asiatics wherever he liked, or confine them to specific areas or jobs, or deport them: discrimination that was 'simply based on colour and race' would be unchallengeable.

Federated Australia was not truly independent and was for many years happy to stay that way. The White Australia policy was the one visceral object of Federation and it was put in place immediately; immigrants had to pass a language test (any language: when the government wanted to ban a left-wing European intellectual, they tested him in ancient Gaelic.)[2] The early federal laws excluded Asiatics and Aborigines from old-age pensions, housing benefits and federal employment. Even in 1914, when the First World War was declared (for a cause that can hardly be described in retrospect as glorious), the prime minister announced that Australia would defend Britain 'to our last man and our last shilling,' and sixty thousand young Australians died in agony on the beaches of Gallipoli or in the trenches of the Somme. So it is anachronistic to see the Australian constitution in any iconic sense as the work of Australians: it was the work, more accurately, of unevolved Australians who were hooked intravenously to British blood. And in the class-calcified Britain of Queen Victoria there was no talk of human rights.

———

Constitutions form a contract between the people and their government, containing express limits upon the powers that the state may exercise over individuals. The Australian constitution, however, is chiefly concerned with limiting the power that the federal government may exercise, not over citizens but over state governments, and little of liberty went into it. The little that did has since proved unsatisfactory. For example, part of Section 80 reads: 'The trial on indictment of any offence against any law of the Commonwealth shall be by jury'.

Our founding fathers intended this as a guarantee that nobody would be convicted of a serious criminal offence in any way other than after trial by jury. Many First Fleet convicts owed their lives to juries mercifully refusing to apply the death penalty which, by the harsh law of the time, was the punishment for stealing goods worth more than 40 shillings. Jurors would undervalue the proceeds of the crime, reckoning them at, for example, 39 shillings, in order to save the thief from the gallows. Mercy was shown by juries to so many that this became one reason why transportation to Botany Bay was a necessary measure to clear the prisons.

You would think that a nation thankful for the mercy of juries would make the right to jury trial fundamental. But the High Court has held that Section 80 guarantees juries only for 'trials on indictment', which are trials under a particular technical legal procedure. In any event, Section 80 does not apply to the states, under whose laws most crimes are tried. It would be simple for the federal government to order that trials – even for murder – should come to a non-jury court by a different legal procedure. As Chief Justice Garfield Barwick remarked, in a case where jury trial had been denied, 'What might have been thought to be a great constitutional guarantee has been discovered to be a mere procedural provision.'[3] No government has bothered to replace it by a statute that would enshrine what most Australians, were they asked, would recognise as the most valued protector of their liberty.

Or take the right to vote, fundamental to any democracy. It seems guaranteed by Section 41, which reads:

> No adult person who has or requires a right to vote at elections for the more numerous House of the Parliament of a State shall, while the right continues, be

prevented by any law of the Commonwealth from voting at elections for either House of the Parliament of the Commonwealth.

Surprise, surprise – this does *not* mean that Australian citizens have a right to vote. It means, according to the High Court, that only if you were alive in 1902, when the Franchise Act was passed, do you have an enforceable claim to vote in federal elections. People whose votes are guaranteed by Section 41 are long dead, so the section itself is now, quite literally, a dead letter. However, in an important High Court case in 2007 brought by an Indigenous prisoner, Vickie Roach, with the support of human rights lawyers acting free of charge, the High Court, influenced by human rights jurisprudence from Europe and Canada, decided (narrowly, at 4–2) that the constitution's establishment of representative government implied a right to vote, at least to the extent that the government could not unreasonably deny it to any class of citizen. So it struck down a Howard government law that prevented all prisoners from voting, although the court admitted it would be powerless to stop the government disenfranchising a narrower class – for example those sentenced to more than three years.[4]

Section 116 of the constitution prohibits federal parliament from 'imposing any religious observance' (although the states may do so) or 'prohibiting the free exercise of any religion' (although the High Court has held that this does not extend to protecting conscientious objectors from conscription).[5] Ironically, Section 116 states, 'No religious test shall be required as a qualification for any office or public trust under the Commonwealth', which is a fine principle until you realise that it is blatantly breached by making the British monarch, who can only be an Anglican, our head of state. The Australian constitution is in this respect a contradiction in terms, although if the matter ever came to court, presumably the head of state would be considered an office or trust over the Commonwealth – the one person who is above the law of the land.

And that is it. There is no right to free speech – although the High Court some years ago found an 'implication' to this effect, more conservative Howard-appointed judges resist constitutional implications and may in time reverse it. In any event the implication only applies to speech about politicians, not businessmen or public servants. There are a few minor rights – Section 92 gives everyone a right to cross state borders and Section 117 says you cannot discriminate against someone because they are from another state, for example, they are Tasmanian. But none of these carry any right to damages if they are breached, so they are, quite literally, worthless.

Do white Australians occupy the country by way of some bargain with its original inhabitants? No such luck – certainly for them. Aborigines were initially treated with compassion, but soon after Governor Phillip's departure the massacres began. First at Risdon Cove in Van Diemen's Land, where in 1804 a large party of Aborigines hunting game was murdered by grapeshot fired on the orders of Dr Jacob Montgarret, Launceston's magistrate. He recovered many of the bodies, melted them down and crammed the bones into casks which he sent, for anthropological amusement, to his colleagues in Sydney. Other massacres followed, and in Tasmania – let's make no melted-down bones about it – the British committed genocide. Although the term would not be coined for another century, the British knew exactly what they had done: they had, admitted a parliamentary committee in 1839, left 'an indelible stain'.[6]

There was to be no deal come Federation. Read the debates and realise how most of the founding fathers spoke of Indigenous people in the same breath as they spoke of kangaroos: as fauna that threatened their crops. Because they viewed Aborigines as sub-human, and certainly as sub-Australian, they refused to count them in the census. As Robert French, Australia's chief justice, puts it, this 'starkly reflected the absence of any place for Aboriginal people under the constitution and the absence of any concern about them on the part of those who were to form Australia's first national government'.[7]

Britain's 'indelible stain' soon became Australia's – its states determined to breed out 'degenerate' Aboriginal genes by a policy of miscegenation, which meant taking girls from their families to service white households and be impregnated by white males. A. O. Neville, the enthusiastic English eugenicist (played by Kenneth Branagh in Phil Noyce's film *Rabbit-Proof Fence*), became 'protector of Aborigines' in Western Australia and boasted that degenerate traits would be bred out within three generations.

His vicious race theories were adopted by all states at a conference in 1938. After the war, Neville's 'eugenicide' was no longer acceptable: it transmogrified into the policy of forcible assimilation that led to the Stolen Generation scandal, for which the Australian prime minister belatedly apologised on 13 February 2008.

Aborigines still have no constitutional rights and may be victims of constitutional wrongs. Section 51.XXVI was amended in 1967, but the Commonwealth was still permitted to enact laws with respect to 'the people of any race for whom it is necessary to make special laws'. This does not mean for their benefit, however. The section was introduced, so Edmund Barton told a constitutional convention in 1897, to enable the government 'to regulate the affairs of the people of coloured or inferior races who are in the Commonwealth'. Even though the purpose of the 1967 referendum was to remove constitutional discrimination against Aborigines, the special laws that can be enacted, for example for the 2008 intervention in the Northern Territory, can be detrimental and discriminatory.[8]

Australia's treatment of its Indigenous people contrasts starkly with other progressive nations, most embarrassingly with that of New Zealand, where the Treaty of Waitangi set the stage for a productive relationship with Maoris. They have four, and may soon have seven, designated seats in parliament, their language is taught in schools and they have a long-established tribunal to deal fairly and impartially with their native title rights. In these respects, New Zealand is well in advance of Australia.

—

Should Australians care that they have few real constitutional rights, that they are reigned over by persons carrying the genes of a long-dead German aristocrat, that their government has special powers to enact racist laws but no settlement with descendants of those who have lived here for so many thousands of years.

The atrocities are in the past, and the founding fathers' failures are well recognised. In many cases their antiquated constitution has been made to work by inventive and activist High Court decisions and sensible agreements that avoid expensive duplicity of Commonwealth and state functions. But, unlike other countries, the federal government offers no legal guarantee to its citizens of rights to live free from torture or inhumane treatment; to speak freely and meet with whomever they choose; to have fair trials held in open court before independent and impartial judges; to enjoy a measure of privacy for home and family life; to be free from oppressive searches and seizures of private property; to be presumed innocent until found guilty; or to live free from discrimination on grounds of gender, race, ethnicity or sexual orientation. If laws of the Commonwealth breach these basic principles – and sometimes they do – there is no basis for challenging them.

Does this really matter? As far as freedom goes, Australian governments have a reasonable record. Besides, agitation for constitutional change is usually uphill. Referenda rarely pass: in 1988 even a 'motherhood' amendment to the Australian constitution, proposing to extend the right to religious freedom and trial by jury to the states, was defeated. A bill of rights tabled by Attorney-General Gareth Evans in 1984 was withdrawn after Queensland Premier Joh Bjelke-Petersen claimed it would permit homosexuals to run naked in the streets and frighten the horses, and Western Australian Premier Brian Burke claimed it would diminish the power of state governments. Whenever change is canvassed, voters are easily convinced that they live in the best of all possible worlds where, if it ain't broke, it ain't worth fixing. When the sun shines and the beach beckons, a better world is difficult to envision, and too much bother to build. Those who do bother seem whingers and spoilsports, importers of problems or, even worse, lawyers.

Whether this complacency is sensible is easily tested. Our government's policy of allowing indefinite detention of asylum seekers has been condemned by the UN and is contrary to international law. The International Labour Organisation found that the Howard government's 2006 Work Choices package breached Article 23 of the Universal Declaration by denying workers the right to have their trade unions engage in collective workplace bargaining. Anti-discrimination laws in Australia do not fully protect people with disabilities, nor do they provide sufficient sanctions to deter unlawful conduct. The High Court has held that there is nothing in Australian law to provide redress for victims of Stolen Generation policies because our law does not guarantee due process, equality or freedom of movement.[9] Anti-terror laws have revamped sedition as a dragnet to chill free speech, which is in a worse state here than in most other democratic countries, with no protection for journalistic sources and no adequate public interest defence to defamation. The judicial enquiry into Dr Haneef's case showed how easily an individual's right to liberty could turn to putty in the hands of a panicked and unthinking government minister. Although federal parliament is debarred from seizing a citizen's property other than on 'just terms' – defined by international law as compensation that is 'prompt, adequate and effective' – most states are under no such constraint (and the referendum question to apply the guarantee to the states in 1988 was comprehensively defeated).

What about the common law – that much prized body of judge-made law inherited from the English, and developed by the Australian judiciary? It has been kept up to date by 'activist' judges, who have created effective rules for contract and commerce, and for resolving disputes over property. But for judges bred in its traditions, freedom of speech and assembly were antipathetic to the right to reputation (however unmerited), and the right to wealth. The common law offers little protection to those on the margins – the homeless, the disabled, the mentally ill. The former federal human rights commissioner, Professor Brian Burdekin, who conducted inquiries into homelessness and mental illness, described the common law as 'an abject failure ... far from being part of the solution, it was frequently part of the problem'. His commission found that 240,000 mentally ill Australians, unprotected by either common law or parliamentary statute, suffered 'scandalous violation of their rights, including hundreds of deaths' largely as a result of government omission, neglect or indifference.[10]

There are a few headline-grabbing examples of the systematic failure of constitutional law to protect human rights. Beneath them, it may reasonably be suspected, lie tens of thousands of incidents of humiliation and disrespect shown to citizens by persons in authority. In a 2007 report, the Tasmanian Law Reform Institute told how it was:

> deeply affected by accounts of the disregard of the basic rights of people with disabilities, the homeless, Indigenous Tasmanians and members of gay, lesbian, bi-sexual, transgender and intersex communities. People with intellectual disabilities informed the Institute about the lack of dignity and respect with which they are routinely treated even by service providers and those charged with safeguarding their interests. They spoke of disregard for their wishes and their exclusion from decision-making about matters affecting them, such as accommodation and health-care provision. They mentioned restrictions on their access to legal services, medical services, entertainment, finance, shopping and employment that have little to do with their needs, capabilities and rights and more to do with the convenience of others. They frequently expressed concerns about personal safety and said that they enjoy a lesser level of protection from physical violence than other members of the community. Consistently they told us of the exploitation of their position of vulnerability.[11]

We have come a great distance, but not far enough, since our forbears left Plymonth in 1787. There is no excuse for permitting law-abiding sections of the population to live as unhappily as this, if their misery can be abated by reforming the law in way that is consonant with our culture and our values. If we can locate and state those values, they can be incorporated into a charter of liberty.

Australia's record on human rights is not bad, but it could be much better. We are a good international sport, signing up to UN treaty bodies, but we refuse to walk when they give us 'out'.[12] A bill of rights was no use in Stalin's Russia or Mugabe's Zimbabwe, but in Rudd's Australia, where it will be enforced by an independent and impartial judiciary, it should have real and positive benefits, especially if we take the opportunity to express in it some deep-seated Australian values, which children could be taught to appreciate and immigrants could be required to endorse. It would be an opportunity to include a commitment to the rights of our Indigenous people, by celebrating their historic place on our land and in our imagination.

A bill of rights is not a panacea for all ills and should not be over-hyped, but it would contribute measurably to better governance.

4

Advance of Fair Australia

On 26 January 1788 Captain Arthur Phillip disembarked from the brig *Supply* at Sydney Cove and watched as a makeshift flagpole was wedged into the muddy foreshore and the Union Jack hoisted high upon it. By that symbolic act of the British Crown, the common law of Britain notionally came ashore and spread its tentacles across the entire continent. This was a result of the legal rule that colonisers automatically brought with them all the law suitable for the conditions of their colony.[1] For subsequent generations, this was a measure of good fortune, for the law of Britain was at that time in advance of any other colonising nation. The previous evening, Phillip's ships had sighted two much grander vessels, captained by the Comte de La Pérouse and flying the flag of France, a country where suspects were routinely tortured by judicial warrant, where Catholicism was compulsory and the notorious *lettre de cachet* put any critic of King Louis XVI immediately behind bars. British law was the best of a bad lot: it outlawed 'cruel and unusual punishments', for example, although the lash (cruel but usual in the Royal Navy) was soon to reverberate throughout this open prison. Nevertheless, Phillip did his best to acknowledge such rights as the law permitted, demonstrating by his own 'first law', 'that there can be no slavery in a free land and hence no slaves', a commitment to liberty well ahead of his time.

What legal rights did British law bestow on these bedraggled soldiers, convicts and, in due course, settlers, as they huddled under wattle-daub twelve thousand miles from Westminster? There was Magna Carta, the 'great charter', the first treaty to circumscribe, if only to a small extent, the absolute power of the sovereign, and to promise, 'To no man will we sell, to no man will we deny or delay, justice or right.'

Phillip brought habeas corpus as well, although there was little call for it at first: the convicts were lawfully detained because they had been convicted. Of more use were the free-speech rights recently secured by John Wilkes. There was no immediate call for trial by jury (convicts and soldiers alike faced court martial) but emancipists would soon make it their first demand.

This, then, was the patchwork quilt of common law that the First Fleet brought with it to the great south land – a law primitive in many respects, but shot through with piecemeal recognition of some fundamental rights. And although the reason for settlement was prison overcrowding, it was not uninfluenced by the theory that bad characters could reform in a different environment. In so far as the penal settlement had a beneficent ideology, it was that of Christian reformers who believed that a London villain might yet make it to heaven through a life of hard work in a place where there were few unconsidered trifles to be snapped up. This was a moral vision of considerable naivety: officers and prelates recount how they were continually taken in by convicts fraudulently claiming to have 'turned over a new leaf'. In the long term, however, the experiment succeeded, notwithstanding the jibe by Winston Churchill (who disliked Australians) that we had 'a recessive convict gene'. We can take moderate pride in the fact that we are the only advanced nation to have been founded, and for the next seventy years partly peopled, by criminals. *Les Misérables* brings tears to the eyes of theatre audiences around the world by tunefully retelling Victor Hugo's moving account of the reformation of a thief, but the Australian story is exactly this, writ large.

So what old British rights have had a special relevance to Australia, and what new rights have been born from its own unique history? Since charters can serve as symbols of national unity and as templates for teaching national history, what of relevance to liberty can be found in the origins of the colony and its subsequent struggles?

—

Outstanding in the minds of those who decided to found this far-off prison and keep it supplied with convicts for the next seventy years was that the sentence of transportation was not a sentence of indefinite detention. That they considered morally wrong, so they offered 'the ticket of leave' as a promise of liberty in the event of good behaviour. It is ironic that for all the limitations in the moral vision of those British politicians and penologists, they were capable of discerning an evil to which modern Australian cabinet ministers have turned a blind eye: indefinite detention occurred at Guantanamo Bay, and it could happen to asylum seekers and their children at detention centres here. (The High Court, in a 2004 case called *Al-Kateb v. Godwin*, found no basis for interpreting immigration law in a way that would prevent the indefinite detention of innocent people.)

Australia can be proud of having shed the class divisions that still scar its progenitor, which were rampant at the time of the First Fleet. For all that Britain had contributed to liberty by 1788, its electorates were gerrymandered, power was in the hands of corrupt or incompetent court favourites, over 150 minor offences were punished by hanging and in London alone there were 50,000 prostitutes, many of them children. The grinding poverty of the time comes down to us now in the paintings of William Hogarth and in the poetry of William Blake, who had the moral vision to see the tears of chimney sweeps, to hear the curses of London harlots and to feel the cruelty done to children in the poor house. Wealth was inherited: there were no dole-bludgers because there was no dole to bludge. It was a time, Oliver Goldsmith reminds us, when 'laws grind the poor, and rich men rule the law'. You were born in a certain rank and station in life, and expected to stay in it. You were assigned, as the nursery rhyme says, to be either: 'Tinker, tailor / Soldier, sailor / Rich man, poor man / Beggar man, thief.'

British life circa 1788 was a costume drama for which the costumes were handed out at birth. But in the colony, these class distinctions were gradually eroded. The early examples – soldier, convict, free settler, squatter – eventually disappeared: convicts earned tickets of leave and were joined by gold diggers from many nations. Wealth and status were, in due course, open to all men, or at least to all men's children. Ironically, our first patriot, William Charles Wentworth, who was the offspring of a highwayman and an emancipated convict woman, and who devoted much of his life to agitation for trial by jury, press freedom and self-government, later turned reactionary and demanded that the country be ruled by a 'bunyip aristocracy' based on wealth.[2] We have the rise of the trade unions, and some liberal lawyers, to thank for quashing Wentworth's oligarchic ideas.

The professions remained more difficult to access until, much later, Commonwealth scholarships opened up the universities, although there are still bastions of private-school snobbery and barriers to women's progress. But, by and large, the nation's refusal to adopt the British class system is something to celebrate. The bill of rights should pronounce anathema on all forms of discrimination – not only race and sex discrimination (firmly outlawed under federal legislation) but discrimination based on sexual orientation or national origin or family connections or wealth. The law should be no respecter of persons, as the Levellers famously put it in a draft of an early bill of rights, their 1647 Agreement of the People:

> That in all laws made or to be made, every person may be bound alike; and that no tenure, estate, charter, degree, birth or place do confer any exemption from the ordinary course of legal proceedings whereunto others are subjected.[3]

——

What can we find worth celebrating today in a bill of rights about the arrival of 1300 convicts and their guards on the shores of Sydney Harbour? There was a prescient moral vision in Arthur Phillip's attitude towards the Aborigines. The Colonial Office knew there would be 'Indians' – sharp-eyed Lieutenant Zachary Hicks, who first descried the coast of Australia from the crow's nest of the *Endeavour* at 6 pm on 19 April 1770, soon caught glimpses of their fires. But the British government, misled by William Dampier's assumptions about the natives he had seen on his voyages that reached the Western Australia coast, thought the Aborigines were nomads who could stake no claim to the country over which they transited. The land in this sense was believed to be *terra nullius*, and its Indigenous people, who had in fact been settled in certain areas for fifty thousand years, had no greater rights to the country than the kangaroos. They were expected to blend back into the scenery – the First Fleet, unlike other colonising voyages, carried few trinkets with which to bribe or to buy the inheritance of the original occupiers.

Thus our colony of thieves did begin by an act of theft. But it's not fair to say that there was any intention to subjugate or oppress the Aborigines. Read those old Home Office reports now, couched in the language of the British civil servant throughout the ages, and what comes through is a kind of 'live and let live' philosophy: the great south land is big enough for us all (except, of course, for the French). The prime minister, that workaholic bachelor William Pitt, had ordered that no wives should accompany the convicts – as one wag put it, 'He did not intend to allow felons a luxury he denied himself.' Men outnumbered women by 7 to 1 so Governor Phillip was ordered by the Home Office to procure brides for them from amongst the natives and the women of the South Seas – the little penal colony was planned as a multi-racial society from the outset. Of course, things didn't work out that way. Phillip did not have the heart to bring wives from New Caledonia to share the misery of the first years, though he became so worried about an outbreak of sodomy that he threatened any suspects with the most devastating fate imaginable – then or now – a one-way ticket to New Zealand.

The First Fleet was a Noah's Ark of nationalities. There were prisoners from Europe and America, lots from Ireland and nine West Indian convicts and cooks. Many convicts, and Governor Phillip himself, had Jewish ancestry. His dream of founding a new nation (a belief derided by others at the time) is the dream that came true. His sense of fairness was extraordinary for the age and the place. He insisted that Aborigines be treated humanely and with recognition of their innate dignity – a vision astonishing for his time, and for his position as a colonial prison governor. In his very first despatch from Sydney he wrote of his 'determination from my first landing that nothing less than the most absolute necessity should ever make me fire upon them'. He kept this resolution, even after he was speared through the shoulder at Manly while looking for Bennelong, whom he had befriended in his determined effort to understand Indigenous culture and to invite peaceful co-existence. That was not a sentiment shared by others, as Phillip wrote six months after the landing: 'Living with the natives – to the officers they were an amusement, to the convicts they were people inferior even to themselves. They all tried to take their own wrongs out on the black man or to make what profit they could out of him.'

He ordered convicts who had been harassing natives to be flogged in front of the tribe. But he was outdone in compassion on that occasion: the Aborigines, appalled at the calculated brutality they were witnessing, began to whimper and weep and beg for the punishment to stop. Phillip was not taken in, as was James Cook, by the romantic ideal of the noble savage – some tribal rituals were barbaric even by the standards of the British navy. What he showed in his actions, and recognised in theirs, was a common bond of humanity that distance, time and spiritual beliefs could not disguise.

A symbolic gesture was made at the first meeting with curious Aborigines at Botany Bay on 22 January 1788. The party of marines was ordered to pull down their trousers and show they were men, not gods, who shared the same mortal organs of human reproduction. (Modern feminists might interpret this historical moment differently – as the first limp assertion of dominance by the new Australian male.) It is not known what the Aborigines thought as they were vouchsafed sight of these white and wrinkled scrota: their own would, in years to come, be cut off and dried and used by early settlers as pouches for tobacco. Phillip's moral vision did not long survive in the colony after his departure in 1793, but it is there, in our history – a standard of decency and justice briefly set, and worthy of commemoration.

Recognition in a bill of rights of Arthur Phillip's brief period of compassion would not, of course, make up for what followed: the brutal massacres, the virtual extermination of Tasmanian Aborigines and the attempts to 'breed out' what were officially described as 'degenerate' Aboriginal traits in the inter-war period. This was followed by the era of the Stolen Generation, a policy, to put it bluntly, of well-meaning genocide. These unforgettable and unforgiveable wrongs are there in our history and cannot be whitewashed by saying sorry, although considering the long and truculent refusal by the former government to say that simple word, its utterance by Mr Rudd in 2008 was historic. What will follow? A treaty giving legal rights of co-existence? Our Indigenous people have a place in any Australian statute of liberty, which must recognise not only their rights to equality and due process, but their special status as original owners and occupiers of the land. Moreover, a domestic bill of rights should not only celebrate a nation's achievement of liberty, it must not shrink from memorialising injustices of the past, by providing rights that will stop them from recurring.

Phillip's first law against slavery was soon forgotten in order to give farmers and squatters their bondsmen – the convicts who provided free labour for seven years in order to earn a ticket of leave. When better bred English families arrived in the colony, it was usually to receive ample grants of what had become Crown land, along with convict servants and labourers, over whom they had power to administer floggings (their victims would hobble with broken backs for months after the lash had removed their flesh).

Governor Macquarie's worthy experiments with reformation – he advanced emancipists and even appointed several as magistrates – were hotly opposed by free settlers, whose selfish attitudes and increasing wealth made them an incipient upper class. Macquarie's levelling instincts were disfavoured by a British government that refused to end transportation: it was not until the gold rush in 1851 that the secretary of state realised, 'It would appear to be a solecism to convey offenders at the public expense, with the intention at no distant time of setting them free, to the immediate vicinity of those very gold fields which thousands of honest labourers are in vain trying to reach.'[4] So it was ridicule rather than humanity that stopped the traffic in bonded labour, but the folk memory of the brutality that attracted tourists to 'Old Sydney Town' can be reflected by a rule against torture and inhumane treatment.

Australia has no revolution to celebrate in its liberty bill – no fights for independence against kings or tyrants or colonial powers. But this does not mean we lack the experience of struggle. The settlement in its early decades was marked by intense struggle – first to conquer the vastness of the ocean with its constant dangers, and then against the hard, unyielding environment, against starvation and disease and aching loneliness in the bush. Read the diaries of the First Fleeters to understand just how close Sydney town came to becoming a ghost town. Read about the arrival of the second fleet with its human cargo – five hundred of them brought ashore dying or seriously ill. Phillip's insistence that the First Fleet should not sail at all until it was properly provisioned, his foresight in taking on board the fresh fruit that prevented scurvy, and his insistence on sharing rations equally between officers, soldiers and prisoners, were all decisions attributable to a humanity that was far ahead of his time. In memory of it, we should opt for a statute of liberty that includes economic and social rights to a basic minimum guarantee of food, shelter and medicine. These are also the very rights the Australian delegation helped to engineer into the Universal Declaration: including such rights in a liberty bill would be an appropriate way of monumentalising this diplomatic achievement.

There is a feature of Australia's early history that resonates with more recent economic and social concerns over climate change and the environment. It is the astonishing achievements of scientists – navigators, geographers and cartographers, botanists, naturalists and hydrographers – who charted the great south land, and collected and exhibited its unique flora and fauna, introducing the world to kangaroos and lyre birds, koalas and platypi. William

Dampier was first to bring back samples of flowers and wattle in 1688 (they are still held at Oxford University) but much of the credit belongs to Joseph Banks, who funded his own scientific team on the *Endeavour* and was first to explore Botany Bay. The samples and drawings he took back to tantalise the Royal Society are now in the Natural History Museum of London (which no longer bothers to exhibit them). If these amazing collections were returned to Australia, as they should be, together with the collection sent to England by Banks' protégé Matthew Flinders, we might perhaps see the point of including a right to protect and enjoy the environment to which these men dedicated years of their lives to understanding.

It was Matthew Flinders who suggested the name 'Australia', after circumnavigating the continent and producing charts so accurate that they were still used in the Second World War.[5] In 1802 he encountered the ships of the French scientific explorer Nicolas Baudin, at a place in South Australia named, in consequence, Encounter Bay. Twelve thousand miles from their countries, which were locked in desperate war, these two scientists breakfasted together and eagerly shared the geographical and anthropological information they had each accumulated in their research of our southern shores. It was a 'Copenhagen' moment, in which the quest for scientific truth overrode national hatreds.[6] The knowledge they were sharing was, of course, of pristine and astonishing surroundings: they had pressed its flowers for further study and captured its unique marsupials, in nets and in drawings and diary descriptions.

The determination of these heroic explorers to understand the beauty of a fabulous land, setting off from what Phillip described as 'the finest harbour in the world, where a thousand ships of the line could ride in perfect safety', could be also be remembered in this right to preserve our environment. A right to be free of visual desecration features in many national bills, and Australians have more need of it than most. We were powerless to stop NSW politicians approving the building of 'the Toaster' and Blues Point Tower and the Cahill Expressway, which spoil views of the finest harbour in the world. The enjoyment of our natural surroundings should be an entitlement and not merely an opportunity.

We are fond of recalling our medical pioneers, men such as Howard Florey, virologist Frank MacFarlane Burnet and ophthalmologist Fred Hollows, and scarcely a month passes without some internationally important discovery being made at an Australian university or research institute. One of the most brilliant breakthroughs in the last thirty years has been the role of Australian scientists in pioneering IVF treatment, although their work in Victoria was for a long time hampered by outdated laws. Joseph Banks was responsible for Australia riding to prosperity on the sheep's back, studying samples of wool from the colony and arranging for Merino sheep, smuggled out of Spain, to be sent to Macarthur and Marsden in Sydney.[7] To the memory of these, and other scientific and social pioneers, the right to engage in ethical scientific experiment could be dedicated.

The right to fair play has a long ancestry in the colony. As soon as the emancipists achieved a political voice, they raised it in favour of trial by jury and the right to sit on juries. It was granted after a lengthy struggle against governors who wished to keep the court-martial system (which made conviction a near certainty), and colonists, who were horrified at the thought that those accused of robbing them might be tried by men who once robbed others. The emancipists' fight became the main civil liberty issue in the 1820s.[8] As we have seen, the victory was not entrenched in the Australian constitution – the apparent right to trial by jury turns out, as a result of deceptive drafting, to be merely a procedural provision. The role of 'the gang of twelve', whose sympathy verdicts saved many a prisoner from the gallows, should figure in any statement of the liberty of Australian citizens, namely the right not to be imprisoned for over a year other than through the verdict from twelve good men and women true.

'Mateship' is a much touted Australian tradition, of uncertain origin, although it probably goes back to the goldfields and entered folklore for real in the great strikes of the 1890s, such as the shearers' strike of 1891, which led to the formation of the ALP, and inspired both 'Waltzing Matilda' and Henry Lawson's warning 'They needn't say the fault is ours / If blood should stain the wattle!'.[9] Tom Keneally sees mateship at its best in 'Weary' Dunlop succouring POWs brutalised by the Japanese on the Burma railway (and at its worst in pack rape). It can be brought home in a charter by reference to the struggle to combine for a better working life through the right to join trade unions and to associate for legitimate common purposes. We should remember the Eureka Stockade of

1854, when twenty-five diggers from the gold mines, who had demonstrated against the oppressive licence hunts by burning their prospecting licences, were butchered by mounted troops. This was blood on the wattle, spilt by a government in Melbourne that refused to acknowledge these men's right to protest against injustice. Its conduct was all the more outrageous because the diggers – 10,000 of them at a mass meeting – were demanding an end to police corruption, the right to vote (then limited to holders of more property than they possessed) and the right to stand for parliament. Although the shameful blood-letting hastened these democratic reforms, the memory of those who fell at Eureka can be honoured by the right to free association in an Australian statute of liberty.

This right can also pay tribute to the Tolpuddle Martyrs, the embryonic trade unionists who were convicted in Dorset in England for swearing a secret oath and transported to Botany Bay in 1834 – our most celebrated non-Irish political prisoners. Later in the century Australian trade unions struggled to establish themselves, and their role has been clouded by their early racial obsessions. (The first strike, by the Seaman's Union in 1878, was over the employment of Chinese crew). However, their achievements are worth celebrating because throughout the twentieth century they were ahead of their time: they fought for a minimum wage, a forty-hour week, paid holidays, long-service leave and the fabled 'smoko'. In time Australia's progress in protecting its workers made us a valued member of the International Labour Organisation and we contributed to its campaign for human rights at work, outlawing child or sweated labour, racial and sexual discrimination, inequality of pay, and the denial of the right to join trade unions and have them collectively bargain. The fact that this last right was denied by Work Choices provides a very good reason for entrenching it in a statute.

The rights of suspects should be protected in a country with a longstanding apprehension about the police, deep enough to turn a bush terrorist like Ned Kelly into a folk hero. 'Jihad Ned' killed an informer and three coppers in cold blood, then planned a rail crash that would have killed eighty more of them, along with innocent women and children on the same train. His plot was foiled by a brave school teacher, Tom Curnow, who risked his life to warn the engine driver. So who was the hero? You may well ask, since Curnow's name is forgotten and Ned Kelly has become an icon.[10] It took decades of abusive conduct by state police forces to produce such mawkish sympathy for an obviously guilty cop-killer. So a liberty bill that sets out the basic rules for the fair treatment of suspects of crime would benefit the police as much as suspects.

These are necessary rules to guard against the conviction of the innocent through confessions procured by bashing them up, or by trickery or unfair inducements. Australia has had its fill of miscarriages of justice: a case that famously illustrates the dangers of leaving a vulnerable suspect in police hands without these rights is that of Rupert Max Stuart, the Aborigine who was sentenced to hang in 1959 in South Australia for the murder of a young girl. His improbable confession was allegedly browbeaten out of him, in the absence of lawyer or interpreter, and his neck was only saved by a newspaper campaign appealing to the better nature of South Australians run by Rupert Murdoch (the young Rupert Murdoch). Max Stuart is still alive – a leader in the outback – and represents a small class of innocent men saved by newspaper proprietors in need of a circulation-building story. There are many others who have gone unjustly to the grave, or to a lengthy term of imprisonment, who would have been saved had greater attention been paid to the rules of human rights. Dr Haneef's four-week ordeal at the hands of incompetent politicians, and policemen who turned a blind eye to the evidence of his innocence, would have been cut very much shorter had those rights been in place.

Australia should be proud of its establishment in the 1870s of a free education system, compulsory at primary and early secondary level. This took a leaf from the schoolbook of the Gladstonian era of improvement, but was introduced with a genuine Australian characteristic: the country school teacher who became the backbone of the bush community. Secular state education gave rise to religious reactions: Protestant churches set up their own schools to inculcate the fear of God, at least in the sons and daughters of the rich. Catholics, at the time predominantly Irish, were concerned that secular state schools might imperil their hold over the souls they wished to save and the version of Irish history they wished to teach, so they set up an alternative system. In time, universities were established, which offered tertiary education to all who merited it by way of Commonwealth scholarships. The rights that are worth celebrating here are, first, everyone's basic right to free and secular education until the age of sixteen; second, a right to be able to access higher education on the basis of merit; and, third, the right of parents to opt out of state education for their children, and to enrol them in schools that conform to minimum educational standards set by the state.

Although education is regarded as a 'second generation' right, these three propositions appear both uncontroversial and enforceable against, say, an education department that arbitrarily refuses to approve a particular private school, or that fails to make adequate provision in state schools for students with learning difficulties. Their enforcement would be a welcome reminder of the purpose of education, and would justify the closure of schools that teach race or religious hatred. And it would fulfil the promise of Article 26.2 of the Universal Declaration:

> Education shall be directed to the full development of the human personality and to the strengthening of respect for human rights and fundamental freedoms. It shall promote understanding, tolerance and friendship among all nations, racial or religious groups, and shall further the activities of the United Nations for the maintenance of peace.

There is little in early colonial Australian history – or in later Australian history, for that matter – that suggests any determined commitment to free speech. Nothing to show that we share the passion of the republican poet John Milton, who famously likened plans to censor the press to 'the exploit of that gallant man who thought to keep out the crows by shutting his park gate'. He cried, 'Give me the liberty to know, to utter and to argue freely according to conscience above all liberties.'[11] British juries would sometimes take a stand against the government's attempts to suppress its critics. Londoners chanted 'Freedom of the press' after booksellers were acquitted at the Old Bailey of selling Tom Paine's *The Rights of Man*. This may have encouraged Australia's first chief justice, the courageous and remarkable Francis Forbes, to stem the stream of seditious libel actions brought against early newspaper editors, and to strike down Governor Darling's attempt to control the Sydney press by declaring that Darling's new press laws amounted to a 'prior restraint' repugnant to the laws of England. Forbes regarded a free press as 'indispensable in a free state because of its tendency to counteract that eternal propensity of our social natures to make slaves or dupes of one another'. Although he doubted its fitness for a 'state of society where one half of the community is worked in chains by the other', he did his best to thwart Darling, a narrow-minded military martinet who could not bear criticism.[12] In commemorating Francis Forbes, more advanced than his modern brethren both in his commitment to free speech and his disdain for wearing wigs in hot climates, we should also spare a thought for Edward Hall, editor of *The Monitor*, jailed repeatedly by other judges for his seditious libelling of the stiff-necked governor.

Otherwise, there were few blows struck for liberty of expression: in 1951 Frank Hardy was arrested for criminal libel in *Power without Glory*, and Cyril Pearl's *The Wild Men of Sydney* (1970) had to be bought in Brisbane lest the wild men's relatives sued in New South Wales. Moral censorship was all the rage in Australia's unswinging sixties: Prime Minister Menzies refused to allow *Lady Chatterley's Lover* to be imported after its Old Bailey acquittal because (as he told cabinet) he did not want his wife to read it.[13] It was not until 1992 that the High Court discovered that a right to say what you honestly believe about politicians might be 'implied' from a constitution that established democracy, and even then the 'implication' did not extend to protect honest speech about anyone else, no matter how powerful.[14] So be careful what you say about big bad businessmen or irresponsible bankers; and environmentalists, please note how criticism of corporate executives can provoke a storm of writs.

In 2006 an authoritative press freedom index ranked Australia thirty-ninth in the world, lower than Britain, New Zealand, Costa Rica, Bulgaria, Estonia and Trinidad. In that year we had not only a libel law without a proper public interest defence, but a thousand suppression orders on supposedly 'open court' proceedings, journalists convicted and threatened with jail for refusing to disclose sources for important news stories, and new suppression powers in anti-terrorism sedition laws.[15] These laws threaten journalists with up to five years in jail if they criticise ASIO operations, or refuse to reveal their source for a story about terrorism. Whistleblowers who tell the media about matters of great public importance are prosecuted, and secretive ministers have found ways to neuter the Freedom of Information Act.[16] In 2006, much to Australia's embarrassment, the Human Rights Committee condemned the country for violating freedom of expression by requiring a police permit before anyone could make a speech on matters of public interest in a public space that was used for this purpose. The High Court had abjectly failed to recognise any right of robust public debate, despite a stinging dissent from Michael Kirby.[17]

So there seems nothing much to celebrate by a free-speech guarantee, other than two centuries of political lip-service to the concept and the reality that, thanks to libel damages, although we do not have free speech in Australia, at least we can have expensive speech. However, freedom of expression has always been regarded by human rights courts as the most fundamental of freedoms – the UK Human Rights Act has a special clause giving it particular prominence – and into the liberty bill it must go, with added protection for freedom of information and the principle of open justice.

5

The Case for a Statutory Charter

An Australian charter will not merely lay down universal standards, or improve the quality of our jurisprudence, or provide a modern method for courts to interpret parliament's statutes and regulations. It should define the freedoms that have an important place in the Australian story. It should have a preamble that school children can recite with pride; its guarantees should be stated clearly and non-legalistically, in a language that every citizen (and every migrant) can understand; it should reflect universal standards, topped up by values that Australians, through their experience and their imagination, hold especially dear – values such as the importance of fairness, enterprise, equality, advancement on merit, and the moral imperative of paying our debt to Indigenous Australians.

Australian public life has always reverberated with the rhetoric of liberty. Every prime minister and premier has boasted that we are as free, or freer, than any other country in the world. Freedom was the reason for fighting the Second World War, in which so many young Australians lost their lives. Australia was one of the first of twenty-six allied nations to sign the Atlantic Charter on 1 January 1942, expressing itself as 'convinced that complete victory over their enemies is essential to defend life, liberty, independence and religious freedom, and to preserve human rights and justice in their own lands as well as in other lands'. What is this, other than a promise to the men and women in the war effort – many of them now in nursing homes or struggling with diseases of mind or body – that government will do its best to ensure that they and their children and their children's children will live in a land where liberty, as defined by progressive conceptions of human rights and justice, will eventually flourish? Given the Anzac pride in this promise, delivered with such sacrifice, why the reluctance to incorporate it in a charter?

Resistance to change is instinctive: 'If it ain't broke, don't fix it' is an idiotic argument against improvement, which would have us still flying about in DC3s, driving golden Holdens and playing LPs. The case for standing still, for avoiding change even when it is going on all around us, plays on our insecurity. It enjoins us to 'Always keep a-hold of nurse / For fear of finding something worse.'[1] It can only be refuted by a commonsense assertion that familiar arrangements can be changed, and for the better. In making this assertion, the odds must be calculated as scientifically as possible: by comparative study to see whether the change has worked well for other similar societies; by careful assessment of how it might work for Australia; by predicting its broader consequences; and by asking how it comports with the history of the nation and its present needs. While rhetoric has its place in any debate – especially about matters of liberty – it is important to be accurate.

There have, unfortunately, been many exaggerations and misstatements by opponents of an Australian charter. Wild claims have been made about the effect other charters have had on their countries, especially on the UK. The truth is that after over ten years of operation in the UK, the Human Rights Act has proved of particular benefit to law-abiding citizens, protecting them from unfair or insensitive civil servants. It has not produced an avalanche of cases to clog up the courts or politicise the judiciary. There is evidence that it has worked to promote a much greater awareness of the need to respect human dignity. South Africa (with constitutional guarantees for liberty) and New Zealand (with statutory protection) have almost two decades of experience, and are generally reckoned to be the better for the existence of their bill of rights. Canadians adopted a statutory charter in 1960, but were sufficiently satisfied with its operation to have it adopted as part of their constitution in 1982. European states – all forty-seven of them – subscribe to the European Convention on Human Rights: they have accepted the rulings of its court at Strasbourg, usually without demur, and in consequence have been able to change their laws for the better.

Some nations, of course, have bills of rights that do not function, either because they are mere propaganda exercises (for example, the Soviet Union under Stalin) or because they have lickspittle judges who will not enforce them against the government (Zimbabwe under Robert Mugabe). However, there is nothing in the experience of democracies comparable to Australia to suggest that a bill of rights would be a backward step, and increasing evidence shows that it improves the services provided by government, the quality of parliamentary discussion and the political awareness of citizens.

There are now three recent and comprehensive assessments of the case for and against Australian state bills of rights, conducted in Victoria, Tasmania and Western Australia. They involved wide-ranging consultation with members of the public, as well as with experts and community organisations, and all reported that such a statute, although necessarily limited and local, would have a range of beneficial effects without any serious downside. The Western Australian report, in late 2007, by a consultative committee chaired by Fred Chaney, is particularly thorough and convincing.[2]

The ACT adopted its Human Rights Act in 2004, and Victoria followed with a charter in 2006. Canberra resounded in 2004 with dire predictions about what the opposition leader described as 'potentially the most dangerous legislation we have ever seen', which was going to flood the courts, enrich lawyers and lead to a judicial takeover of government. Five years on, these predictions appear comical. There has been very little litigation and the Liberal party opposition has learnt to love the new law, at least by invoking it increasingly in parliament as a standard for holding the government to account. The main impact, a recent study reports, has been on the policy-making and legislative process, because it has spotlit human rights issues and inspired debate on them, both among the Executive and in the Legislative Assembly.[3] On issues ranging from practices in youth detention centres to prisoners' voting rights, the use of children for test-purchasing tobacco, the wearing of headscarves in schools, strip-searching powers, procedures at inquests after bush-fires, treatment of public-housing tenants and penalties for tree removal, the act has informed and enlivened parliamentary debate and executive decision. This shows it is contributing to a healthy democracy in the territory: it may have more effect on administration when amendments requiring public authorities to comply with it come into force in 2009.

The Victorian charter too has produced few court cases, but has had a galvanising effect on parliament's ability to identify and debate human rights issues. The government conscientiously attaches lengthy 'compatibility statements' to every new piece of legislation, although unsurprisingly they invariably conclude that the new bill passes the test, or else that any incompatibility is reasonable in the circumstances. Occasionally this rings untrue: for example new powers have been given to coroners to close their inquests, in breach of the open justice principle. These powers should be capable of challenge by the press, although the Victorian charter only allows individuals – not media corporations – to take action. Thus broadcasters could not use the charter to object to the injunction in the state against the television series *Underbelly*, a fictionalised account of gangland killings in Victoria, banned lest Victorian juries learn from it that (surprise, surprise) there have been lots of gangland killings in Victoria.[4]

There are other defects in the charter: it does not apply to courts or tribunals acting in their judicial capacity (and they are the very first bodies to which it should apply), and it provides no right to damages, even for serious charter violations. This is unsatisfactory: it may be that damages should be capped (I have suggested at $50,000 in my draft bill), but justice requires that individuals who have their rights violated should be compensated for the terrible stress this can cause, often over a period of years.

A recent study of the charter's impact on the legislative process in 2007 found it had sparked and informed debate on no less than ninety-three bills. The Victorian Equal Opportunities and Human Rights Commission asked:

> If it was not for the charter, would the human rights dimensions of these ninety-three bills have been identified, analysed and debated? In all but a very few cases, the answer is clearly 'no'. For this reason alone, the initial impact of the charter is significant: it is already comprehensively expanded the parameters of public policy analysis to include the transparent assessment of new laws against a human rights framework. This is a substantial achievement.[5]

It would have been even more substantial if the commission could show that any of these debates had led to government defeats or withdrawals of inconsistent legislation, but it is early days. And the government's willingness to provoke criticism of its bills by flagging human rights implications, which might otherwise go unnoticed by the opposition, bodes well for its receptiveness to future declarations of incompatibility.

One recent case in Victoria demonstrates the value of a court-enforced charter. The government had, quite irrationally, refused to accept autism as a disability for the purposes of providing special educational services. A mother with an autistic child who had been deprived of those services sought the assistance of employed lawyers in the Human Rights Law Resource Centre in Melbourne, who took her case to court, claiming a violation of the charter, with overwhelming evidence that autism was a disability that deserved special assistance for children at school. A fortnight before the case was to come up for hearing, the government conceded its mistake and provided extra funding for autistic children.[6] This is exactly the kind of case that shows the charter can work to improve the quality of life of vulnerable people who, through no fault of their own, are unfairly disadvantaged.

Critics claim that a bill of rights helps only minorities, especially minorities that are feared or disliked, such as prisoners or asylum seekers. If so, this should be welcomed: the true test of a society is the way it treats its most vilified members. But in fact, the prime beneficiaries are ordinary citizens who have been victims of unfair treatment by malign or careless bureaucrats, in matters ranging from government misuse of personal data to arbitrary or irrational refusals by local councils to allow their ratepayers the freedom to make improvements that do not bother their neighbours. For a society such as Australia, which embraces the notion of a 'fair go' for even its most vulnerable members, how can this be a bad thing?

Some of those whose better treatment is secured by a bill of rights are indeed 'minorities' – in the sense that they are very young, or old enough to be in nursing homes, or sick enough to be in hospital. We were all young once, and will in due course become old and incapacitated: what on earth is wrong with insisting that such groups be accorded a degree of dignity? Those who oppose a bill of rights in the knowledge that it will help vulnerable people, whom moral duty and Christian charity demand we help, appear neither moral nor Christian – and sadly, in Australia, opponents include a number of churches.

In 2007 the Australian people evinced a desire for change by sweeping from power a prime minister adamant in his opposition to the progressive trifecta – a republic, a treaty with Indigenous people, and a bill of rights. In 2008, Prime Minister Kevin Rudd's 2020 conference gave general support to all three reforms. The ripeness of this time for their implementation has been called into question by those who argue that making better provision for liberty should take last place to dealing with other pressing problems, such as terrorism, economic meltdown and social problems in remote communities. However, a better definition of liberty is relevant to dealing successfully with these very problems.

Terrorist attacks upon Australians have been made by Islamic extremists imbued with a fervour for universal sharia in a form that breaches many human rights standards. To deter potential sympathisers, it is not only necessary to denounce terrorism but to explain why the values that the terrorist wants to inflict upon society are unacceptable. A secular bill of rights does that, by endorsing universal standards, which put religion exactly where it belongs in democratic society; by upholding an individual's right to believe what he or she wants to believe and granting reasonable facilities for undisturbed worship without impinging on the rights of others to worship other gods, or none at all; and by allowing anyone to be an apostate, and to live in a society where women and homosexuals are treated equally. Human rights stand for tolerance, and expose by comparison the terrorist's extreme version of Islamic fundamentalism, primitive in its sexism and barbaric in its punishments. At the same time, enforceability of the fair trial and treatment provisions in the charter, and its promises of non-discrimination, will provide some security for peaceful Islamic communities in Australia, more confident that their own rights will be protected and their members will not, as Dr Haneef was, be made the victims of unfair procedures and false accusations.

A bill of rights has other related uses, for example in the context of immigration, where it can provide a yardstick when considering applications for permanent residence, naturalisation and asylum. Why should we accept for settlement any person who is not prepared to embrace the freedoms his or her desired country of residence is pledged to uphold? John Howard and Peter Costello were constantly making the point that refugees and migrants should accept 'Australian values', but they never had an authoritative statement of those values to hand.

This was additionally regrettable for Alexander Downer when he sought to chide other nations for breaching standards that Australia supports but has never legally endorsed. The Pacific has been an area of particular concern, with the regular overthrow of democracy in Fiji and resistance to it in the Solomon Islands, not to mention problems in other island nations involving widespread domestic violence against women, discrimination on grounds of race against Indians and tribal outsiders, and the corruption of judges and bashing of prisoners. Fiji even features an utterly discredited Human Rights Commission, which exults in the expulsion of newspaper editors and pumps out propaganda for the army dictatorship. Once Australia has put a charter in place, it can take credible initiatives in a region that has no court or other mechanism for monitoring or condemning human rights abuses.

—

When money markets and banks around the world are collapsing, and a recession is having serious consequences for employment and production, need we concern ourselves with human rights? Emphatically yes, because this is when human dignity becomes more important than ever. In Australia there must never be Hoovervilles – the vast camps filled with men thrown out of work by the Great Depression in the US. In times such as these, economic and social rights become particularly important in the distribution of basic commodities, and delivery of health care and housing to the poor. Civil and political rights guard in desperate times against victimisation and scapegoating of races and minorities. They help to ensure that government intervention in the economy is fair to all citizens, for example with the rule that nationalisation of property should take place only on just terms. This is the one human rights rule that is fully reflected in the Australian constitution, and hence is the best known (probably due to the plot of the movie *The Castle*). It is not a rule, however, that exists in all state constitutions.

The judges of every nation have a duty, as far as they are able, to keep the law they enunciate up to date and responsive to the contemporary needs of the community they serve. In this task, cases decided in other advanced countries are often helpful. Such decisions are not binding, of course, but they may be 'persuasive' (in other words, influential). The decisions that have carried most weight in Australia have been British common-law judgements, which were followed blindly by Australian courts until 1963.[7] Other helpful decisions come from New Zealand and South Africa; the US Supreme Court is accorded respect, and occasional reference is made to Canadian case law. This process has always worked both ways: the courts of these countries are open to influence from Australian judicial decisions as well. This exchange of precedents is how new legal concepts and legal theories, inventive ways of settling new problems and disputes, even judicial aphorisms, get disseminated through the global community. Australia has produced some outstanding judges: Sir Owen Dixon was regarded as the best common lawyer of his time, and if there had been an Olympic team medal for judging (and since there are such medals for taekwondo and beach volleyball, why not?) then the High Court presided over by Sir Anthony Mason would have won gold throughout the 1980s. But that was before the great human rights resurgence, when bills of rights in South Africa, the Caribbean, Canada, Britain and New Zealand began to produce a new kind of jurisprudence.

By the dawn of the twenty-first century, the most important and far-reaching debates and developments in the highest courts of all advanced countries except Australia concerned the application of human rights principles – not only constitutional and criminal law, but contract and torts, medicine and media, personal injury and equity, social security, immigration and town planning. It is an intellectual development in which Australian jurists cannot play a significant part, simply because they have no bill of rights to interpret and apply. This should be a matter of real concern to Australian lawyers, and the chief justice of New South Wales has expressed anxiety about our intellectual isolation from developments in other countries with a shared common-law heritage.

It should concern non-lawyers as well. If we had outdated ethics that prevented our scientists from undertaking important experiments being conducted by their colleagues in other countries, or if bureaucratic regulations prevented our businessmen from freely competing with foreign rivals, or if enhanced coaching techniques for sport were unavailable here so our athletes always came last, these defects would be addressed immediately as matters of national importance. So, too, with the law: it is time to drag it into the present day, so our judges can contribute to the development of human rights and equip themselves to produce better jurisprudence and justice. No longer would cases be decided by reliance on old precedents, they would be decided on first principles. Decisions based on first principles are more comprehensible: people who are not lawyers can understand the reasoning. Adjudication by reference to the principles in a bill of rights is better adjudication: more logical, more commonsensical and more satisfactory in result.

Judges express irritation when their judgements are misunderstood by the media, but they often write at excessive length, in convoluted language, which obscures the real issues, so they appear to reach results on technicalities rather than on merits. Anyone who doubts this should compare two cases in which the important question of whether governments can detain foreigners indefinitely without trial was decided. One was judged by the top court in Britain with the help of a bill of rights (they ruled 8–1 against indefinite detention); the other by the top court in Australia without a bill of rights (they ruled 4–3 in favour of indefinite detention).[8] What stands out, when the two decisions are compared, is the clarity of reasoning in the English case and its preferable result, which one member of the Australian majority who upheld the indefinite detention wished he could reach, if only he had a charter to guide him. The defendant in the

Australian case, Ahmed Al-Kateb, had committed no crime. He actually wanted to leave the country and return to either Kuwait or Gaza, but no state would accept him and he was therefore imprisoned indefinitely under the policy of mandatory detention and at the expense of the Australian taxpayer. This result was reached in a convoluted set of disparate judgements totalling over 50,000 words, with details incomprehensible to most who are not lawyers and many who are.

The clarity of the decisions the courts make is important, and the excessive length and complexity of Australian High Court decisions is a real problem. In one way, this is understandable given there is so much case law around now, which judges feel bound to quote and discuss. But the public needs to comprehend judicial decisions and lawyers need clarity so that they can advise their clients in the future. A bill of rights would, in many cases, enable the court to avoid lengthy discussions of previous cases and begin anew by applying charter principles to the facts in simple and straightforward language. In this sense, a charter can help Australians reclaim their law from judges, who would be required to set out their reasoning from first principles rather than old precedents, in a way that could be understood by intelligent laypersons if it were published in a journal or the review section of a Saturday paper. Some judges will doubtless find this suggestion quite shocking, but it is notable that candidates for the highest court in England (the Supreme Court, formally the House of Lords) are now required to display an ability to write reasonably short and intelligible judgements.

This is an aspect of a citizen's right of access to the courts: not only must they be open to all with genuine charter grievances but they must produce decisions intelligible to citizens who are not lawyers.

A statute of liberty involves a choice that each society must make for itself. The fact that other advanced societies have come down in favour, and have not been minded to repeal their bills since enacting them, does not prove conclusively that such a bill is a good and workable idea for Australia (though it does prove it is a good and workable idea for advanced democracies). The evidence from Britain over the past decade provides many examples of how and why a statute can supplement gaps in the common law. Of course, it has thrown up some hard cases and there has been a degree of uncertainty about new rights – one being privacy. In one case a mentally disturbed young man decided to commit suicide and did so late at night, cutting his wrists in a city centre in front of CCTV cameras. He was rescued and later recovered. The local council and the police thought his case would be a good example of the advantages of CCTV, and a television company made a programme that used the CCTV images. The man objected to his moment of anguish being shown on television. The courts in England thought the public interest outweighed his right to privacy – his suicide bid was, after all, made in a public place. The European court held that the value of broadcasting these pictures was insufficient reason to expose an individual's moment of intense mental torment.[9] The two competing views are equally arguable, but surely it is better to live in a society with a law that allows the argument to take place, than to live with a common law that allows no argument at all, because it offers no remedy for breach of privacy.

There is a great deal of literature – sociological and statistical – confirming the positive impact of a national bill of rights on constituting and maintaining national identity. The constitution is the most important symbol of civic identity in America, its rights providing the people both with their guarantee of democratic government and with a guarantee that government will not encroach on their liberties. As one commentary concludes, the constitution with its bill of rights 'is our pre-eminent symbol of nationhood and the doctrine of judicial review is a major practical support for both the attitudinal and the behavioural elements of the American civil culture'.[10] Similar conclusions have been drawn by Canadians about their charter of rights: Pierre Trudeau added it to the constitution for the avowed purpose of creating a unified sense of being 'Canadian' (by thinking of themselves as right-holders, Trudeau reckoned, Canadians would be encouraged to see themselves as a single people and to resist the separatist pull of Quebec nationalism). The charter seems to have served this purpose: surveys suggest it quickly became popular and was viewed as having strengthened Canadian identity.[11]

Of course, Americans define themselves as the heirs of the founding heroes who forged their bill of rights, and Canadians with no particular history to be proud of have found a new constitutional institution on which to base a national identity, namely the liberal and democratic principles of their charter. Care must be taken in extrapolating from other countries with very different histories, but the US and Canadian experience does provide some reason to think that Australia, too, may draw inspiration and national identity from a charter that offers citizens a set of values perceived as distinctly Australian and (in the case of those that are universal) are proudly seen to be enforceable in Australia, unlike so many other countries that proclaim them then violate them.

If the charter is rooted in the dignity of the individual, irrespective of his or her ethnic, cultural or religious background, and is taught in schools, promoted in workplaces and enforced in courts, there is reason to think that it would become a force for national unity in our multi-racial and multicultural society.

———

One vexed question, answered in different ways by different nations, is whether a charter should include economic and social rights. These are the rights to which Australia has creatively contributed – and has been ahead of most other countries in so doing. The trade union movement ensured that before other countries we had a basic wage, a forty-hour week and an arbitration system that recognised rights at work. This has brought reasonable disability benefits, superannuation and other forms of social security. Medicare and medical benefits, while not universal or uncontroversial, nevertheless provide medical cover that citizens of the United States, for example, would envy (however much they might wish to avoid the conditions in some of our hospitals). Those who advocate inclusion only of civil and political rights overlook the fact that these are difficult to 'enjoy' if you are starving or wracked with disease, or lack the education to know they exist. The survivors of Auschwitz I have met remember the camp as a place not of powerlessness or disentitlement but of constant and agonising hunger.

Most contributors to Fred Chaney's inquiry in Western Australia wanted economic and social rights included in their charter, especially those people and organisations in rural areas (the further they were from Perth, the worse the provision for health and educational services).[12] The problems of enforcing them seem to have been exaggerated: public interest litigation in India and Canada is frequently brought on behalf of people denied access to sanitation, medical care or university education. A World Bank study found that these cases did not involve judicial trespass on government prerogatives.[13]

The most suitable comparator is South Africa, which put social and economic rights in its post-apartheid constitution. In 2002 its constitutional court required the government to make a new anti-retroviral drug available to HIV-positive mothers and their newborn babies, to reduce the risk of the transmission of the virus. There were no resource problems because the manufacturer was prepared to supply the drug free of charge for five years, yet the South African government refused to distribute it other than at a few test locations. In a decision credited with saving the lives of many thousands of children, the court ruled that this policy was inflexible and unreasonable, and hence a breach of the constitutional right to health care.[14] By applying the test of reasonableness, the court found a way of enforcing the right: it referenced a recognised legal standard for judging administrative action, which respected government policy choices unless they could be shown to be irrational or unnecessarily discriminatory against the poor.[15]

In another case the year before, which challenged government housing policy, the court declined to debate hypothetical questions such as whether alternative measures might have been more desirable, or whether public money might have been better spent. But it was prepared to intervene if housing policy ignored the needs of the poorest and most vulnerable members of the community.[16] There is nothing in the South African casebook to suggest that economic and social rights would be problematic if placed in an Australian charter.

It is ironic to recall that Dr Evatt's promotion of social and economic rights in the Universal Declaration was initially resisted by Eleanor Roosevelt, on the grounds that Australia, in 1948, was such a progressive country that its standards should not be imposed on other nations. This prime position has not been maintained, to judge from authoritative indices that were published at the end of 2008. The Global Gender Gap Report, published by the World Economic Forum and drawn up by professors at Harvard and Berkeley, examined the gap between men and women in four basic areas: economic participation and opportunity; educational attainment; political empowerment; and health and survival. It ranked Australia twenty-first in the world. Above us are New Zealand (fifth), Sri Lanka, the Philippines, Trinidad and Moldova, as well as the UK and other advanced European nations. We are narrowly ahead of South Africa, Quebec, Lithuania and Argentina, but we are falling (we have slipped from seventeenth in 2007 and fifteenth in 2006).[17] On the World Bank's Gini Index, which assesses the extent of income inequality, we did much worse – we came forty-first, behind Belarus and Bulgaria, Canada and Croatia, Egypt and Greece, Ireland and Japan, and the Ukraine. In terms of the extent of child poverty, the OECD in 2008 rated the twenty-three most prosperous nations and Australia came fifteenth, behind Greece, Spain and Japan and the usual Europeans. Any statistic that draws in our Indigenous people is invariably uncomfortable – we have the second-highest rate of child suicide, above all nations except the depressive state of Finland. Statistics of this sort never tell the full story, but they do identify uncomfortable patterns: we are not comparatively bad, but we are certainly not comparatively as good as we think we are, or as we ought to be.[18]

There is a particular problem with freedom of speech in Australia, and it is important for the media to understand how a bill of rights will ameliorate it. Press freedom is demonstrably ill-served here compared to other advanced countries, where it is protected by a free-speech guarantee. Australian journalists are threatened with jail when they refuse to disclose their sources; there are far too many suppression orders; the public interest defence to libel actions is much more restrictive that in the UK or New Zealand, or any country in Europe. Australian judges, with the notable exception of the first chief justice, Francis Forbes, and the former South Australian chief justice, John Bray, have generally been antipathetic or indifferent to freedom of speech. The High Court under Sir Anthony Mason provided a narrow public interest defence for comments about politicians by discovering an 'implied right of political speech' in the Australian constitution (a discovery for which, ironically, these 'activist' judges are regularly condemned by the very commentators who make most use of it). This implied right is controversial and restricted – it does not extend to comments on business or businessmen, for example, which is why Australian financial journalism is so restrained, nor on any other powerful clique in our society. Why not? Because our courts do not have any charter right to deploy in order to shape the common law of defamation to meet modern needs. British judges have that ability and have used it, and as a result the law that Australia originally inherited from Britain is far more supportive of free speech than it is here.

So why are sections of the Australian press so vehemently opposed to a charter? My impression, after discussion with some editors, is that they have a visceral fear that judges are so hostile to the press, and uncomprehending of the difficulties and deadlines of journalism, that they will in some way use a charter to further disadvantage the media. I share their concern about the inability of Australian judges to comprehend the full meaning of freedom of expression in a democracy – a meaning that began with Milton and carried on, through John Wilkes and John Stuart Mill, to the great case of *New York Times v. Sullivan*.[19] But I do not think the answer for the media is to boycott and abuse courts into which they will anyway be dragged: the better response is to educate judges, and new generations of judges, by way of a charter, in what the liberty of the press really means.

In Britain, before the bill of rights came into force, I found the same judicial incomprehension. It has changed, slowly but surely, as a result of the European Convention and the Human Rights Act. Take the all-important question of the right of journalists to protect their sources – a right that the common law forcefully rejects, and even the US Supreme Court does not accept. In 1996 I acted for a young journalist – Bill Goodwin – who had written a true story about a company's secret plan for refinancing, based on a confidential source. The company hauled him into court and demanded to know the name of his source, whom they speculated (wrongly) must have been a disloyal director, or even a burglar. Despite the existence of a statutory 'shield law' (with exceptions so broad it was no help at all), the judge made the order, threatening the journalist with prison if he did not obey it. The three judges of the Court of Appeal confirmed the order, but offered him the opportunity to put the name of his source in a brown paper envelope, to be opened only if we lost in the highest court, the House of Lords. We refused this poisoned chalice and duly lost 5–0 in the House of Lords. That meant that nine of the best British judges had all decided (correctly, as the law then stood) that journalists and their sources had no protection. We took the case to the European Court, arguing that such protection was essential if newsworthy stories about powerful corporations were to be published by the press as part of its 'watchdog' function to guard free speech in a democracy. These judges – eighteen of them – included jurists from Eastern European countries recently liberated from communist rule, who knew firsthand the vital importance of a press free to probe the powerful, because they had lived so long without one. They handed down a judgement that now protects journalistic sources throughout Europe. It says:

> Protection of journalistic sources is one of the basic conditions for press freedom ... without such protection sources may be deterred from assisting the press in informing the public in matters of public interest. As a result the vital public watchdog role of the press may be undermined and the ability of the press to provide accurate and reliable information may be adversely affected. Having regard to the importance of the protection of journalistic sources for press freedom in a democratic society and the potentially chilling effect an order of source disclosure has on the exercise of that freedom, such a measure cannot be compatible with Article 10 of the Convention unless it is justified by an overriding requirement in the public interest.[20]

This passage is now regularly quoted and endorsed by British judges, sitting in the very courts from where, until

Goodwin v. UK, they would have foamed at the mouth and delivered pompous homilies about the duty of journalists to obey the law of the land. (Indeed, when *The Guardian* tried to protect its source – a young typist in the Ministry of Defence – for an important story about the secret placing of US cruise missiles in England, it was threatened with massive daily fines that would have put it out of business. So it revealed the source, who was then jailed for a breach of the Official Secrets Act).

My point is that judges can – and do – learn from changes in the law. They now understand the reason for protecting sources and they have become quite proud of the fact that British law is, in this respect, more supportive of press freedom even than US law.[21] Australian judges, who have jailed four journalists and fined others over the last twenty years, will, I am sure, change as well once given sensible legal direction by a charter. We will not again have a case such as the one in 2004 when the Howard government prosecuted two *Herald Sun* journalists who wrote a story exposing the fact that the government was secretly planning to renege on a promise of pensions for war veterans. The journalists were threatened with jail unless they disclosed their source for the leak and fined $7000 when they did not. This could never happen in Europe, thanks to the ruling in the Goodwin case.

The editors of *The Australian* do not accept my argument. They distrust judges and believe the only way forward is to pressure the government for statutory change.[22] But after a massive campaign on the subject by the press in Australia in 2007, all Attorney-General Ruddock was prepared to offer was a catch-22 'shield law', which would protect the source only if the journalist could prove that identification would cause him harm: in most cases, this very proof would be likely to identify him! Although the press may have more luck with the current attorney-general, they face another catch-22 – the new shield law will be interpreted by judges who are hostile to its purpose, and to the press. So by all means work for statutory reform, but the only long-term solution is a charter containing the kinds of rights drafted in chapter 8 to create a presumption in favour of media freedom.

The same point applies to reform of defamation law, which has turned the right of free speech in Australia into a right of expensive speech. There is a 'Your Right to Know' campaign to draw its defects to the attention of politicians. But politicians are the last people who want to change libel laws, the winnings from which traditionally go to remodelling their kitchens and installing swimming pools. Reform will come by way of courts developing the common law, with the help of a charter, or reform will not come at all.

Again, the British experience under the Human Rights Act is instructive. The common law of libel has never provided the media with any public interest defence: if they mistake facts or publish truths that their sources will not come forward to verify, they pay damages, no matter how important the story or how responsibly they have acted to research it or to correct it afterwards.

In 1998, as the Human Rights Act was passed, the law lords developed a public interest defence for responsible journalism on subjects of public importance – a defence much wider than the fragile 'constitutional implication for political discussion' permitted by our High Court.[23] Trial judges, bred in the arcane dogma of common law libel, were at first hostile to the new defence and sought to limit its operation. In one case, they held that my client, *The Wall Street Journal*, could not invoke it to defend an important story about Saudi Arabia's co-operation with the US in the war on terrorist financing. The Saudis had (and this was crucial to the story) allowed a leading Saudi business identity to be monitored by the CIA. His libel victory against the paper was overturned by the House of Lords in 2007 in the leading case of *Jameel v. Dow Jones*, when the judges said that this was precisely the kind of responsible investigative journalism that was protected by the new defence, derived by the freedom of expression guarantee and the Human Rights Act.[24] Again, this is a defence that would not be available to any newspaper sued over a similar story in Australia. Ironically, the leading judgement in this landmark decision was given by the same judge who had, ten years before, declared Bill Goodwin guilty of contempt for not revealing his source.

So the moral of my story about these two cases is that charters can and, over time, do change judicial attitudes to favour the freedoms they enumerate. The Human Rights Act has also cut back on the suppression orders that are such a bane for court reporters here.[25] The Australian media would better serve its own interests, which at the end of the day are the interests of the public to be informed about the behaviour of the powerful, if it campaigned for, rather than against, a charter.

6

The British Experience

The UK's bill of rights has become a frequent focus of the Australian debate. Australia for many years faithfully followed British court decisions, even when they were wrong, and we still accord them some influence. Our political system is closely modelled on Westminster's and we have copied many of its political reforms, on the assumption that what improves governance in Britain will improve it here. Both supporters and critics of the charter have drawn on what they claim is the British experience. So it is important to understand both the thinking behind, and the workings of, the Human Rights Act introduced by Tony Blair's government in 1998.

The British, who gave more liberty to the world than any other country, began to fear declarations about rights when they were made by victorious American colonists, and even more when they were made by the French revolution armies. 'When I hear of natural rights,' Jeremy Bentham snapped, 'I always see in the background a cluster of daggers and pikes introduced into the national assembly . . . for the avowed purpose of exterminating the King's friends.'[1] As we have seen, he described natural rights as unprovable and unpredictable – 'nonsense on stilts'. So long as rights were sourced in God or nature, rather than the common law, they frightened the pragmatic English. It was not until Hitler began to extinguish freedom in Europe that in 1940 an intellectual rethink began. H. G. Wells and his committee of middle-class writers and scholars drafted a bill of rights suitable for all 'parliamentary peoples'. They eschewed the messianic natural law preambles of the French and American declarations in favour of the simple observation that, 'since a man comes into this world through no fault of his own' he is in justice entitled:

1) Without distinction of race or colour to nourishment, housing, covering, medical care and attention sufficient to realise his full possibilities of physical and mental development and to keep him in a state of health from his birth to his death.

2) Sufficient education to make him a useful and interested citizen, easy access to information upon all matters of common knowledge throughout his life, in the course of which he would enjoy the utmost freedom of discussion.

3) That he and his personal property lawfully acquired are entitled to police and legal protec-

tion from private violence, deprivation, compul-
sion and intimidation.

And so it went on, in homely if occasionally dated style,
promising among other things: 'there shall be no secret
dossiers in any administrative department'; 'a man's private
house or apartment or reasonably limited garden enclo-
sure is his castle'; 'no man shall be subjected to torture,
beating or any other bodily punishment, or to imprisonment with such an excess of silence, noise, light or dark-
ness as to cause mental suffering or in infected, verminous
or otherwise insanitary quarters'.[2]

H. G. Wells' draft bill of rights inspired Roosevelt's 'Four
Freedoms' speech, and went into the thinking behind the
Atlantic Charter and the Universal Declaration of Human
Rights. Both the Atlee Labour government and its Churchill-
led successor supported a bill of rights for Europe, first
suggested by Dr Evatt at the 1946 Paris Peace conference,
which was drafted by British lawyers and ratified in 1951.
This European Convention on Human Rights was based
on the Universal Declaration and sought to articulate civil
rights threatened by communist regimes in Europe.

It was not until the mid 1960s that the inability of
British common law to deal with new demands for
freedom became apparent to Lord Chancellor Gerald
Gardiner, who accepted the right of individual petition to the European court, giving British citizens an
opportunity, once their claim had been turned down
by the highest court in the UK, to take a final appeal
to Strasbourg. Gardiner also revived the Law Reform

Commission and chose a great judge, Lord Scarman, to head it. Scarman's work demonstrated that British law – inherited by Australia – had yawning gaps in the protection of civil liberty, and he became a powerful supporter of the need for a bill of rights that could be directly enforced in British courts, without complainants having to travel to Strasbourg to obtain redress. The media suddenly recognised the force of his argument when the European court condemned as contrary to freedom of expression the British law of contempt of court, because it had stopped newspapers publishing details of the plight of thalidomide victims, merely because they were in litigation – which had lasted many years – with the drug's manufacturer.[3]

Scarman had little difficulty persuading Conservatives, and the educational force of a bill of rights had long been recognised by influential Labour thinkers. Professor Harold Laski, the leading left-leaning intellectual, pointed out:

> Bills of rights serve to draw attention to the fact that vigilance is essential in the realm of what Cromwell called fundamentals. Bills of rights are, quite undoubtedly, a check upon possible excess in the government of the day. They warn us that certain popular powers have had to be fought for, and may have to be fought for again. The solemnity they embody serves to set the people on their guard. It acts as a rallying point in the state for all who care deeply for the ideals of freedom.[4]

In 1979 the case for a bill of rights received powerful support from Lord Hailsham, the once and future Conservative Lord Chancellor. He analysed the way in which democratic governance now tended towards 'elective dictatorship', as the prime minister and cabinet could effectively rule to their heart's content through a tame civil service, docile majority support in the House of Commons and a powerless parliamentary opposition. When the Thatcher government was elected, however, the bill of rights ceased to be a Tory priority. ('Elective dictatorship' is always less objectionable when you have been elected to power and are doing the dictating.) The Labour party, meanwhile, was split. One faction (and factions speak louder than words) took fright at the behaviour of judges in Margaret Thatcher's union-bashing Industrial Relations Court, and figured that British liberties might be safer in the long run left to independent enforcement by the European Court of Human Rights. This objection receded as home-grown judges showed their independence in striking down unfair government decisions where they could, under their existing powers of judicial review.

In 1993 the Labour party declared its full conversion to the proposal for a statutory bill of rights, and one of the first actions of Blair's government, elected in 1997 on a manifesto that included a promise to introduce a Human Rights Act, was to do just that. It simply adopted the European Convention as part of domestic law, making its provisions directly enforceable in British courts. This meant that judges had to interpret statutes 'as far as possible' to conform to the act's liberty guarantees. What they could not do, however, was strike down any law passed by parliament. All they could do, if the law was blatantly in contravention, was to signal to the legislature that it should be looked at again, by issuing a declaration of incompatibility.

The Human Rights Act was passed by the British parliament in 1998 with all-party support. It made the European Convention on Human Rights, containing all the civil and political rights (but not the economic or social rights) found in the Universal Declaration, a part of the law of Britain. It included an interpretation clause that required judges to construe existing laws as best they could, consistently with the rights in the convention.

There were five main reasons why the act enjoyed cross-party support. Firstly, European convention cases had revealed serious gaps in common and statute law. By 1998 over one hundred decisions in Strasbourg had been delivered against the UK, forcing alterations in the British laws that had failed to protect fundamental freedoms. The path was blazed by Stanley Golder, a prisoner denied by prison rules the right to consult a lawyer. In 1975 his complaint was upheld and the government was obliged to alter the rules so as to allow all prisoners access to legal advice.[5]

Subsequently, European court rulings were responsible for putting an end to in-depth interrogation of suspects in Northern Ireland, the birching of juveniles in the Isle of Man and caning in state schools. They forced liberalisation of the test for contempt of court, providing a public interest defence for editors, permitting journalists to see all the evidence led in open court and allowing the media a right of appeal against suppression orders imposed during trials. Strasbourg judgements required the UK government to provide safeguards for citizens against arbitrary telephone-tapping; ended the prohibition on homosexuality in Northern Ireland; removed certain discriminatory clauses in the immigration rules; secured some citizenship rights for British passport holders in East Africa; required changes in the law to enlarge the rights of mental patients; ensured that parents have access to information on which local authorities decide to take their children into care, or send them to foster homes; upheld the rights of poor persons accused of serious crime to have legal aid extended for their trials and appeals; and gave decisions that played a part in the advent of a Data Protection Act and an Equal Pay Act. Bear in mind that Strasbourg decisions are always cautious: the European Convention on Human Rights embodies basic rather than progressive standards, which must be conservatively interpreted so that they are applied in practice to countries less economically and socially advanced than the UK. All these defeats had become embarrassing to a nation that boasted it was the cradle of liberty.

The second reason the act was passed was because of Privy Council decisions for the Commonwealth. The UK government had granted independence to many Commonwealth countries in the 1960s, and had included a bill of rights in their Westminster-style independence constitutions. Most permitted final appeal to the British law lords in the Privy Council, and by the 1990s these judges had handed down some impressive decisions, protecting liberty in the former colonies with conspicuously more force than they could protect it in Britain when they sat in its highest court, the House of Lords. For example, in 1990 the Privy Council struck down a criminal libel law passed by the Antiguan government and used to prosecute a newspaper editor who exposed that government's corruption.[6] The law lords said that criminal libel was contrary to the guarantee of freedom of expression in the Antiguan constitution – a decision they could not, sitting as British law lords, reach in respect of the archaic criminal libel law in Britain, because the UK had no similar guarantee in a constitution or charter. Such decisions demonstrated both the need to improve judicial protection of British freedoms and the perception that senior judges would be up to the task of interpreting and applying the rules in a charter.

The third reason was the Tiananmen Square Massacre. In 1989 at least two thousand students demonstrating in favour of democracy in Tiananmen Square were brutally mass murdered – by the very Chinese government to which the UK was about to hand over Hong Kong. MPs of all parties clamoured for the immediate introduction of a bill of rights, so that Hong Kong courts could quickly develop a 'human rights culture' and hopefully maintain it after the handover. The Chinese, reasonably enough, pointed out that this arrangement sought to impose upon them civil liberty obligations more onerous than those imposed on the government in Britain. But in the end it agreed to incorporate all the guarantees into a 'basic law', to be adjudicated by a Court of Final Appeal on which a British or Australian judge would sit. Sir Anthony Mason was the first Australian judge appointed to this court, where he was able to enlarge upon liberties that he could not find, except by a somewhat tortuous implication, in the Australian constitution.[7]

The fourth reason for introducing a liberty bill in the UK was the failure of voluntary alternatives. The bumbling Tory government led by John Major in 1992–97 had sought to head off the steam for a bill of rights by announcing a non-statutory alternative, the Citizens' Charter. This document was full of splendid-sounding assertions about the liberty of British citizens, but was soon shown not to be worth the paper on which it was printed: other than encouraging public servants to wear name badges and to answer telephones more promptly, it had no effect whatever.

And the final reason was, simply, that all arguments against a statutory charter in the end collapsed. The basis for the Thatcher government's rejection of reform was that a bill of rights would undermine the principle of parliamentary sovereignty, by which ministers are traditionally accountable to parliament rather than to the courts for the unfair actions of their officials. But it became obvious that this theory had little relevance to the real world of modern party politics, where ministers preside over vast bureaucracies run by unaccountable public servants for whose mistakes they can rarely be made meaningfully responsible. Occasional backbench revolts in the governing party may block a controversial clause in a particular bill, but most MPs cower under the three-line whip. As the Commons debate in the summer of 1993 over the Maastricht Treaty for a tighter European Union dramatically showed, Tory backbenchers viscerally opposed to their government's policy would nonetheless rally to that government if the alternative would be its loss of office (and the possible loss of their seat at the ensuing elections).

By 1998 very few MPs objected to unelected judges having the necessary power to protect citizens' liberties. This argument failed for want of any sensible alternative. The courts remained the only place where oppressive government action against individuals might be checked. The parliamentary opposition does not, by definition, have the numbers to intervene, short of a revolt by government backbenchers. MPs may harass and embarrass ministers over individual cases, they might call for explanations, but they have no power to interfere further. Politicians, moreover, cannot be trusted to champion the liberties of all who elect them. While majority rule resulting from free elections means there is little likelihood that any government would risk electoral reprisals by passing laws depriving the majority of a right they value, minorities remain at risk. Not only unpopular minorities such as asylum seekers or persons suspected of crime, but children, mental patients, homosexuals, the aged and any group insufficiently big to wield electoral power but large enough to attract resentment, or simply indifference.

The notion of parliament as the sole guardian of liberty is risible: three thousand pages of statutes and two thousand separate statutory instruments receive Westminster's imprimatur each year, most of them without proper scrutiny or debate, their contents fully understood only by a handful of administrators and draftsmen. The media, of course, will occasionally take up particular cases of injustice, subject to its ability to obtain sufficient information and to the political allegiance of editors and proprietors. But trial by media – partial, simplistic and usually sensational – can be no substitute for trials by judges.

———

These arguments prevailed, and in 2000 the Human Rights Act came into force in the UK after a fifteen-month period for departmental training to explain to public servants why and how the new requirements for treating citizens with a modicum of decency and respect should be met. Initially, the act was little used in the courts, but gradually, as its provisions were subject to some important interpretations, it settled down and became a routine part of the British legal environment. The Bar, the Law Society and the judiciary are now firmly in favour, as are citizen NGOs and the public service unions.

The press has been inconsistent and simplistic, cheering when the act has influenced a decision that wins media approval (which mostly means a blow in favour of free speech) and booing when it takes the media to task (for example, by pointing out that citizens have a right to privacy). The level of media misunderstanding has been lamentably high, suggesting that of all the classes who need training, journalists are the most in need. Sometimes court decisions that earn tabloid displeasure, normally ones favouring asylum seekers or prisoners, are blamed on the Human Rights Act, when it has had nothing to do with the case. There have been other examples where officials have misunderstood the act, including a police chief who refused to issue photographs of dangerous jail escapees for fear that he might violate their right to 'privacy of home and family life'! Such obvious errors have been quickly corrected, but not before media headlines have shrilly blamed them on the act. As some of these stories have been recycled in scaremongering columns in Australian newspapers, we must take a cold, clear look at what the Human Rights Act has actually achieved in Britain, ten years after its passage.

In the first place, it must be emphasised that the act does not limit the power of a democratically elected government. Where rights are concerned, it actually encourages dialogue about the exercise of power, because the act requires any minister who presents a bill to the House to certify that it is compatible with human rights standards.[8] To assist the minister with this declaration, an all-party committee of parliament has been established (the Joint Committee on Human Rights) to scrutinise all new bills, and to report on their compatibility. If the minister ignores the committee's advice, his decision will inevitably be subject to a debate in both houses. This committee also considers any declaration of incompatibility made by the courts, and advises on whether the offending legal provision should be repealed or amended. In the first ten years of the act's operation, only twenty-six such declarations were made: most were addressed by new primary legislation passed by parliament, when it became aware of the problem spotlit by the declaration. The government, of course, can ignore a declaration of incompatibility, notwithstanding the urging of its Joint Committee: that is what parliamentary sovereignty means. The declaration amounts to a court finding that it is impossible to interpret a statute in a way that does not damage human rights: this remedy will give victims the satisfaction of establishing victimhood, of forcing a parliamentary discussion, and the consolation of obtaining costs.

There has been a technical question raised about the legitimacy of a declaration of incompatibility in Australia, and the issue has been blown out of proportion by certain critics. It derives from the fact that courts refuse to give academic or advisory opinions, or to answer hypothetical questions: they insist on stating and applying the law to concrete factual disputes and providing remedies for proven wrongs. It has been suggested that a declaration of incompatibility may amount to an advisory opinion. This suggestion is wrong, in my view, because the declaration of incompatibility is a remedy like any other declaration and is no more 'academic' than any other question of statutory interpretation. It arises from a specific set of facts and provides the plaintiff with a genuine remedy, namely the satisfaction of establishing authoritatively that his right has been breached, validating his position and requiring the government to think again. It was usually provides him with an award of his legal costs.

Such a declaration has always been regarded by the European Court of Human Rights as an effective remedy providing just satisfaction: all sorts of advantages may follow (favourable publicity, reconsideration by parliament, vindication and sometimes *ex gratia* compensation). The British courts, which refuse to give advisory opinions, have never regarded declarations of incompatibility as 'academic' or hypothetical. In any event, the declaration of incompatibility mechanism is not essential to a national charter – the New Zealand Bill of Rights Act, passed in 1990, has been quite effective without providing the courts with any such declaratory power.

It is, nevertheless, instructive to see what this declaration, which Paul Kelly claims will 'intimidate politicians . . . be divisive, ineffective, damage Australia's judicicary and influence public hostility', has actually done in Britain.[9] Since the Human Rights Act was passed in 1998, up to December 2008, the courts had only granted twenty-six declarations of incompatibility, and eight of these were overturned on appeal. Cases where the declaration had led to an amendment to inconsistent statutory provisions included

- The Human Fertilisation Act (1990): amended to permit a deceased father's name to be entered on the birth certificate of his child.[10]
- The Matrimonial Causes Act (1990): amended to recognise gender reassignment.[11]
- The Mental Health Act (1983): this will be amended so that patients can challenge the appointment of a 'nearest relative' on the grounds that the appointed relative had abused them when they were children.[12]
- The 1861 law in Northern Ireland, which made consensual heterosexual buggery a criminal offence: repealed because it interfered with consensual sexual behaviour between adults.[13]

- The Mental Health Act: amended so that persons who could not be shown to suffer from a mental disorder could be discharged from a mental hospital.[14]
- A section of the Immigration Act, which imposed massive and mandatory fixed fines on trucking companies for unknowingly transporting stowaways: amended so that the penalty could be decided fairly by an independent tribunal.[15]
- An amendment to the Mental Health Act: passed so that persons detained after serving the penal part of their sentence could not have their access to a court blocked by the government.[16]
- Several provisions of the Social Security Act: amended after the courts pointed out, by declaration, that they discriminated against men by providing, for example, bereavement benefits to widows and not to widowers.[17]
- Sections of the Housing Act, which required certain classes of children, and pregnant mothers, to be disregarded in determining priority for council accommodation: amended so that children's needs were always taken into account.[18]

These cases are routine examples of the value of a declaration of incompatibility in spotlighting for the legislature particular sections of acts where parliament has either overlooked an important right or where values have changed since the act was passed. In all these cases amendments were made swiftly, uncontroversially, and indeed willingly by parliament. There was no question of judges 'intimidating' parliament or of the declaration being other than a useful adjunct to democratic governance.

Far from being intimidated by a declaration, in one case, of a prisoner who was refused the right to register as a voter, the government declined to amend the law but announced instead a public consultation on whether and how voting rights might be given to serving prisoners.[19] Another case, which Australian critics such as Bob Carr mention with horror, is the declaration of incompatibility that was issued in respect to the power of the British Home Secretary to fix a jail sentence when a prisoner is given a fixed term of life imprisonment. Such a sentence, which can range from one year to forty years, was previously set in secret by a politician, without a hearing and usually after no more than the briefest flip through the case papers. It was an obviously unfair system and the court declared it was incompatible with the right to have any sentence involving loss of liberty imposed by an independent and impartial tribunal.[20] The government could have demurred and kept the minister's power to sentence lifers, but decided instead to forgo it. The court declaration did not 'intimidate' parliament: there was, on all sides of the House, a recognition that government ministers should not be deciding the length of a convict's imprisonment.

There is nothing, then, in the British experience to suggest that declarations of incompatibility intimidate MPs, or are divisive, or are ineffectual, or damage the judiciary. The most famous declaration was when the House of Lords said that suspected foreign terrorists should not be held indefinitely without charge or trial.[21] Again, the government could have ignored the declaration, but instead it crafted a new regime of 'control orders' – effectively a form of house arrest – that allowed the suspects a degree of liberty, but at the same time ensured the complete protection of the public. In this way, the government was able to solve the law enforcement dilemma while maintaining its principled stance against the indefinite detention of terror suspects by the US at Guantanamo Bay.

Before the Human Rights Act came into force the British courts were already interpreting statutes consistently with human rights:

> Parliamentary sovereignty means that parliament can, if it chooses, legislate contrary to fundamental principles of human rights . . . the constraints upon its exercise by parliament are ultimately political, not legal. But the principle of legality means that parliament must squarely confront what it is doing and accept the political cost. Fundamental rights cannot be overridden by general or ambiguous words . . . in the absence of express language or necessary implication to the contrary, the courts therefore presume that even the most general words were intended to be subject to the basic rights of the individual. In this way the courts of the United Kingdom, though acknowledging the sovereignty of parliament, apply principles of constitutionality little different from those which exist in countries where the power of the legislature is expressly limited by a constitutional document.[22]

The act serves to strengthen the presumption that parliament's words are consistent with the basic rights set out in the convention, and gives the courts an express direction to interpret them in that way 'so far as it is possible'. This remains entirely true to the principle of legality.

The British courts have taken a sensible approach to the question of whether it is possible to interpret statutory language in this way, not only when the words are ambiguous, but when the purpose of the rule they lay down is compatible with a human rights solution. For example, parliament's purpose in passing the Rent Act was to allow an occupant to remain in his rental property as a tenant after his or her partner had died. Originally protection had only been given to a 'spouse', i.e. a married partner, but a later act extended that to include long-term unmarried partnerships – 'a person who was living with the original tenant as his or her wife or husband shall be treated as the spouse of the original tenant'. Parliament's purpose was clear and compassionate: those in long-term relationships would not have to face the prospect of being thrown into the street by a cruel landlord, in addition to their grief at their partner's death. One such landlord, Mr Ghaidan, wanted to do precisely that to his tenant, Mr Ghodin-Mendoza, on the death of his partner with whom he had lived in a London flat for seventeen years in a stable and monogamous homosexual relationship. The law lords held that the act protected the long-term lover: he was a 'person' and he was living in a relationship comparable to that of a wife or husband, even though it was a homosexual relationship. This interpretation was 'possible' because it achieved parliament's purpose of extending the protected tenancy to long-term partners. And so it went with the grain of the parliamentary purpose, even though parliament did not have long-term homosexual partners in mind when it passed the legislation.[23]

Australian critics of a bill of rights have singled out this case for special condemnation, claiming it allows the courts to give *Alice in Wonderland* interpretations ('When I use a word,' Humpty Dumpty said in a rather scornful tone, 'it means just what I choose it to mean.'). They fail to explain the facts, which demonstrate that the decision makes perfect – indeed common – sense. So much so that when parliament came to consider the question a year later, it endorsed the court's decision by passing the Civil Partnership Act of 2004, which gave homosexual partners the opportunity to formalise their relationships.

How successful has the UK Human Rights Act been? Studies in 2006 by the British Audit Commission and the British Institute of Human Rights conclude that its operation has led to better government and better public services: it has assisted decision-makers 'to see seemingly intractable problems in a new light', especially in helping the vulnerable to a better quality of life and protecting them from abuse. A review after five years by the Department of Constitutional Affairs reported that the act has 'significantly improved the development of public policy' and exerted a 'positive and beneficial' impact on the development and delivery of public services, leading 'to a shift away from inflexible or blanket policies towards those which recognise the circumstances and characteristics of individuals'. The review records 'a significant but beneficial impact on the development of policy by central government', leading to better policy outcomes by promoting greater 'personalisation in the delivery of public services and ensuring that the needs of all members of the UK's diverse population are appropriately considered'. The review concludes that the act worked beneficently on policy formulation in three ways:

- By the process for ensuring compatibility with convention rights, through the requirement of ministerial statements and scrutiny by the Joint Committee.
- In response to litigation, which may force a change in policy or its delivery.
- Through changes in behaviour driven by the immediacy of the act, which makes it unlawful for public authorities to act in a way incompatible with convention rights.[24]

The report gives examples of individual cases – of the kind that rarely attract media attention – where the act had improved the life of ordinary law-abiding citizens. For example:

- A couple, married for sixty years, were separated by the local council when they could not look after themselves, and were sent to separate care homes. The act required the council to reunite them.

- The children of a woman in hospital were appalled to find that she was required to eat her breakfast while sitting on the toilet. They complained, citing the HRA, and this indignity stopped.

- Mental patients who sought to be discharged were routinely required to wait six months before their application was even considered, for no reason other than 'administrative convenience'. This practice was stopped by an HRA application.

- The courts have used the HRA to require local councils to show respect for the right to home and family life by maintaining all housing stock in a condition fit for human habitation and not prejudicial to health.[25]

- Courts have required 'special handling' regulations for wheelchair bound people to be less restrictive, and have rewritten them to comport with dignity.[26]

The Lord Chancellor has spoken of 'the hugely beneficial effects of the Human Rights Act' and pointed out that 'very many of the beneficial effects come from the fact that the state, whether it be central government departments or local authorities, now have to consider things in the context of: "Does what I do affect people to the minimum in terms of infringing their human rights?" And human rights mean peoples' basic entitlement to dignity.'[27]

In 2008 the British Institute of Human Rights released a study of the first ten years of the Human Rights Act. Once again, it demonstrated that the act's main use was in protecting vulnerable people from abuse and from poor treatment by public services. It reported that the act has become 'an invaluable tool for public service staff, service users and their advocates, enabling people to challenge poor treatment without having to go to court, because it requires public services to consider people's basic human rights in their everyday work, and to respond to individual needs'.[28]

Its case studies revealed how groups and individuals were beginning to use human rights law, often without the interposition of lawyers, because its language and ideas had inspired and empowered them to cite human rights to challenge poor treatment and to negotiate improvements in their public services. Yet very few of the cases in which they had been invoked had actually come to court, because the public servants involved had changed or ameliorated their conduct. For example:

- A hospital consultant discovered that one of his elderly women patients was crying most of the day because she was unnecessarily strapped into her wheelchair. This conduct ceased when he pointed out that it amounted to inhumane treatment.
- Social workers had invoked the act to request a council to provide special accommodation for a woman and her children at risk of serious harm from a violent ex-partner. The council at first refused, then changed its decision when advised that it had an obligation under the act to ensure that the woman was not treated inhumanely and that her life was not put at risk.

- Prison governors have been required to ensure that black and Asian prisoners are not placed in cells with known racists.
- Mothers with mental health problems who had been placed in residential care have been permitted visits from their children that had previously been denied.
- A disabled woman who needed a special 'profile' bed asked, and offered to pay, for a double bed so she could continue to sleep next to her husband of many years. But a council denied this request and arbitrarily insisted that she should sleep alone in a specially provided single bed. Within a few hours of invoking her right to family life under the Human Rights Act, the decision was reversed.
- A number of cases where older couples had been split up unnecessarily by local authorities into separate care homes, in one case after sixty-five years of marriage, were reversed as a result of greater attention to the right to respect for family life.

There have been many other cases where law-abiding citizens have succeeded under the act in obtaining remedies and relief for unfair treatment. A land owner who lost his property by operation of law as a result of its lengthy possession by squatters was held to have suffered a form of expropriation without compensation, and he was entitled to have the property returned or the full value reimbursed.[29] Then there was the case of a retired engineer who had lived happily in his home in Reading for thirty years, until the local council adopted a new traffic scheme that produced so much noise outside his bedroom window it was impossible for him to sleep. The council refused to pay the cost of insulation and double glazing for his bedroom, but the High Court held that the excessive noise level had breached his right to privacy and he was entitled to £5000 for these costs.[30] This case is interesting because the complainant represented himself: human rights complaints do not need expensive lawyers, or any lawyers at all, because they are based on readily understood principles rather than a multiplicity of case-law precedents.

In other important cases, the courts have given the remedy of ordering an independent inquiry to bereaved families whose children have died in circumstances where public authorities may have been to blame but have tried to avoid any public accountability. In one case, a young Asian boy was placed in a cell with a youth known to be violent and racist, who murdered him. The prison service was relieved of any public inquiry until a court ordered that the 'right to life' provision of the Human Rights Act entitled his next-of-kin to a prompt, effective and independent open investigation so that 'those who have lost their relative may at least have the satisfaction of knowing that lessons learnt from his death may save the lives of others'.[31] This has been particularly important for relatives of soldiers killed on active service abroad, where the courts have insisted, against the army's preference, that there must be full disclosure and an independent inquiry about failures of equipment or supervision that could have contributed to a fatality.

Have there been any downsides to the Human Rights Act? Initially, despite the fifteen-month training period for public servants, there were some obvious mistakes, such as the police chief who made a mug of himself by announcing that the right to privacy prevented him from releasing mug-shots of dangerous escapees. These kinds of errors are now less common, but they do underline the need for training and for assuring law enforcement agencies that the act should not inhibit their work.

The Home Office in 2007 unequivocally accepted that the Human Rights Act 'has not impeded in any way the government's ability to protect against crime'.[32] But there was also an early tendency by ministers and civil servants to blame the act for their own failings. For example, in 2006 the Labour Home Secretary Charles Clarke was found to have ignored his duty to consider dangerous foreign criminals for deportation after their sentences had ended, and it was suggested that the act was to blame, when in fact it was his own and his department's incompetence. Similarly, when a violent offender was granted parole and re-offended, it was widely reported that the Parole Board had released him because of the act. It turned out that the parole board had been advised that the act did *not* require him to be released, but errors had been made in the assessment of his dangerousness.

There have been a number of judicial decisions misreported by the media as turning upon the act, when in fact they have been decided upon entirely different European Economic Community laws. Urban myths have been in circulation as a result of vivid tabloid imagination. It was reported at one stage that the Human Rights Act prevented teachers from putting Band-Aids on pupils who cut their fingers; that the act forces local councils to give land to gypsies. These myths have been debunked in Britain, but they are resurfacing in newspaper articles that oppose a bill of rights in Australia.

—

Most of the anxiety about the Human Rights Act expressed by the British tabloid press is in relation to the new right to privacy. This has to be understood in the context of a media industry that has historically earned its profits by competing for stories about the sex lives of celebrities. The common law puts no break, short of obscenity, on such 'kiss 'n' sell' stories, other than injunctions on what were quaintly termed 'the intimacies of the marital bed': the intimacies of politicians and pop stars in beds other than their spouses' were routinely revealed in Sunday newspapers. The crime of blackmail largely disappeared, as would-be blackmailers found they could make more money by selling the guilty secret they had uncovered to the tabloids.

Elected MPs would frequently become hot and bothered about such privacy invasions (particularly when elected MPs were exposed), but no government dared to support a privacy law because of the power of the tabloids at election time. Support from *The Sun* is credited with ensuring the re-election of John Major's incompetent Tory government in 1992 ('IT WOZ *THE SUN* WOT WON IT' was the paper's own estimation of its power over, and the level of literacy of, its four million readers). Tony Blair had to rush from London to Hayman Island for one day to be vetted and approved by Rupert Murdoch before he won *The Sun*'s support in the 1997 general election.

For many years the entire British press collaborated in playing a confidence trick on its readers, pretending that 'voluntary regulation' by the Press Complaints Commission – a toothless organisation funded and controlled by press proprietors – was effective in protecting privacy. It was not, and various commissions recommended that it should be replaced by a statutory body with teeth for biting, not gnashing.[33] But the tabloids blocked the reform: a junior minister, David Mellor, warned the media that it was 'drinking in the Last Chance Saloon' and was subsequently honey-trapped by *The Sun*, which secretly recorded his sexual trysts with an actress and broadcast them to the nation (literally – his pillow talk was made available on a telephone dirty dial-line).

By the mid 1990s the tabloids had taken invasion of privacy a step further: into the hospital bedrooms of television personalities, who were dying rather than having sex. Donning white lab coats (which get you anywhere in a hospital) and delivering bunches of flowers to patients in nearby beds (with notes inside offering cash for any account of the celebrity's dying words) this was conduct 'up with which we will not put'. It came to a head when journalists from the most odious tabloid (*The Sunday Sport*) invaded the hospital room of Gordon Kaye (star of the TV comedy *'Allo 'Allo*) as he was coming round from brain surgery, and purported to interview him. When his family tried to stop publication of the story, the court of appeal angrily despaired that it had no legal power to do anything, pointing out that the lack of privacy protection in the common law provided no remedy for this outrageous behaviour. It also pointed out that such remedies had been provided by statutes of liberty in the US and throughout Europe, and demanded that parliament consider similar solutions.

When the Blair government was elected in 1997, it decided to leave this thorny issue to the courts, since parliament was plainly incapable of dealing with it. The Human Rights Act 1998 made the European Convention part of British law, with Article 8 providing a right to respect for 'private and family life, home and correspondence'. A clause was inserted at the insistence of the press, which gave special importance to Article 10 (freedom of speech) in cases involving newspapers, and directed the courts to bear in mind any privacy code drawn up by the Press Complaints Commission (this code endorses Article 8 and requires newspapers to justify intrusion into an individual's private life by showing that it is in the public interest to investigate crime or misconduct, or to prevent that individual from misleading the public).

For the first few years of the act, the cases were few (not many individuals wanted the embarrassment of taking a case to court) and not particularly controversial. Jamie Theakson, a TV personality, was secretly filmed in a brothel and could not stop the story about his presence there, but could prevent reproduction of the photographs. Naomi Campbell, secretly pictured leaving a Narcotics Anonymous meeting, could not stop the story itself, which exposed her hypocrisy (she had falsely claimed that she never took drugs), but could obtain modest damages for the publication of the photograph.[34] As long as Article 8 was strictly confined to 'private and family and home life' there was no problem: it stopped the kind of feral journalism that invaded hospital wards, but did not hinder public interest investigations. In 2008 *The News of the World* was tipped off that Max Mosley, the sixty-seven-year-old head of international motor racing and son of notorious fascist leader Oswald Mosley, was arranging a marathon sex session in which five women would be paid to disport themselves as concentration camp guards. It thought itself perfectly within its rights to fit a miniature camera into the bra of one cooperative dominatrix and denounce the whole event on its front pages as a wicked and disgusting Nazi orgy.

Unfortunately for the newspaper, when Mosley sued its story came apart. Its collaborator declined to testify and the judge found, from the evidence of the other happy sadomasochists, that there was no Nazi theme to this private party in a Chelsea basement, nor had it frightened any horses or done any harm other than to the hindquarters of the participants.[35] On that finding Mosley should have been awarded damages for a libel that had continued over six hyperventilating pages of the mass circulation Sunday newspaper, because its journalists had been incompetent. But Mosley sued for breach of privacy instead of libel and persuaded the judge that the paper had invaded his 'private and family and home' life, for which anguish he received £60,000 in damages. This was the right result, but for the wrong reason: disporting oneself in a basement with five hookers is much too remote from that intimacy of personal, family and home life that deserves legal protection under Article 8. News Limited should have won an appeal on this point, but they failed to appeal – presumably because their own behaviour was reckless in seeing non-existent Nazis and they did not want further bad publicity. Some months later the editor of another tabloid launched a bitter attack on the morality of the 'unelected' judge of this case, which fell rather flat: it came out on the day that a comprehensive opinion poll showed the British public had eight times more trust in their judges than in their tabloid newspaper editors.

Rupert Murdoch has sometimes hinted that his British tabloids, which he would not wish his mother to read, are a product of local conditions and sexual aberrations, and are not replicated by his newspapers in Australia. The behaviour of British tabloid journalists when vying for circulation, untrained and unrestrained by any common law concept of privacy, responds to the prurient interest of a readership that devours such stories while hypocritically tut-tutting at their excesses. Whatever you think of the Mosley case (which may depend on whether you think he is a disgusting pervert or not bad for his age) you will probably agree that some degree of privacy should be guaranteed to individuals in a civilised society, and a privacy law developed on a case-by-case basis by judges – the only people who can develop it when MPs will not – is the most satisfactory answer. If they get it wrong an aggrieved newspaper can appeal, so as to ensure that the protection reasonably accorded for personal development of self and family is never used as an excuse to cover up matters about which the public in a democracy should have a right to know.

There are more wholesome examples of benefits that can accrue from a right to privacy. Local councils in Britain recently hit on a new way of making money: by selling their electoral register, which contained personal details, to exploitative direct-marketing companies and consumer credit agencies. They exploited this 'geo-demographic' information to work out specific targets, for example women living alone in particular postal districts, who could then be plagued with telephone calls, or old-age pensioners who could be exploited by door-to-door salesmen. A test case was brought and the court held that although requesting citizens to register to vote was a lawful public purpose, selling their details to commercial concerns was a breach of their right to have a family and home free of the interference that comes of being made a marketing target. Local councils either had to forgo the profit from selling the lists, or permit individuals to 'opt out' by having their name removed. It is precisely because governments, and especially local governments, are prone to take such liberties, without any debate or public discussion, that any charter needs to have a guarantee of privacy.[36]

Debate and controversy over the definition and scope of human rights is to be welcomed, and some criticisms are undoubtedly warranted. But after ten years of experiencing the UK Human Rights Act, no political party wants to go back to a pre-rights era. On the sixtieth anniversary of the Universal Declaration on Human Rights in December 2008, the British prime minister, Gordon Brown, praised the UK Human Rights Act as 'a shield and a safeguard for us all', and Justice Secretary Jack Straw told *The Daily Mail* – a newspaper critical of the act – that its readers do not notice that it 'actually was good in helping to defend the individuals from unacceptable abuse'.[37] There were very few judgements about which he had concerns. He floated the idea that a section on responsibilities might be added to the bill, requiring obedience to the law and loyalty to the country, but this was immediately derided by Nick Clegg, the leader of the Liberal Democrats, as a 'mealy-mouthed sop' to an antagonistic tabloid.[38] Clegg's party wants the act strengthened and amended to include economic and social rights. The Conservative leader David Cameron promises a new British bill of rights with protections for trial by jury and other British institutions. Other rights that have crystallised since the European Convention was drafted in 1950 are being urged for inclusion, such as a right of access to the courts and protection against discrimination on the grounds of age, or sexual orientation, or disability.

In one respect, it might be said that the act has failed: although it has helped vulnerable people to receive a greater level of respect from the authorities and has provided citizens with a remedy against unfair treatment, it has not conduced to the 'culture of liberty' that its proponents wishfully predicted. That is because it is still perceived as

'European'. Despite the fact that it was drafted by Winston Churchill's lawyers it makes no reference to British institutions such as trial by jury (because most European countries have criminal trials by judges) or to the special contribution the nation has made to the advance of liberty. It is not an appropriate vehicle for teaching the human rights story: British children still leave school ignorant of the struggle to abolish torture, or to establish an independent judiciary and the sovereignty of parliament. This is partly the fault of the government, which has not insisted that these momentous events be part of the curriculum and has not bothered to put pioneers of its liberty such as Tom Paine and John Wilkes on statutes or on stamps. (The British establishment is still slightly embarrassed about its radicals: the regicides, after all, established the supremacy of parliament by cutting off the head of the only English monarch who ever cared about culture.) Australians should not be so diffident about celebrating the mavericks who have contributed to their freedoms.

The British experience, properly analysed, provides strong support for a statute of liberty for Australia: it suggests, however, that we could take a lead by incorporating social and economic rights, and by producing a charter that takes account of the most recent international conventions. It also warns that a bill of rights can easily be misrepresented by newspapers editors and commentators; that it should be introduced with training programmes; and should be indelibly Australian, in the sense that it refers back to the rights that the people – especially our people – have struggled to achieve.

7

Critics

A charter that reflects universal, and hence minimal, standards that any decent government must pledge to uphold (pledges that all Australian governments since 1948 have made by ratifying and endorsing UN declarations and conventions) should in theory be politically uncontroversial. After all, the struggle for human rights has been waged by leading politicians and thinkers from both right and left. In Britain the Tory Lord Hailsham argued the need to curb 'elective dictatorship' with a bill of rights, and Tony Blair's New Labour government brought in a charter without Conservative party opposition – the party whose leader is now campaigning for a 'British' bill of rights.

But in Australia the debate has been highly politicised, not only between the two main parties but also within the Labor party itself. The latter critics are led by Bob Carr, former New South Wales premier, and John Hatzistergos, the current New South Wales attorney-general, who object to any shift of state power from elected politicians, or to judges. Since judges already engage in supervision, by way of interpreting and applying those laws, this criticism decodes into a claim that they should not have more power, nor better tools for doing their job, which would be supplied by a statutory bill of rights. This criticism is elaborated by several newspaper commentators, whose vitriolic attacks on judges as a class ('aristocrats', 'juriscrats' and, most damning of all, 'ex-lawyers') find a welcome home in *The Australian* newspaper. A number of academic and commercial lawyers can be called upon for sceptical commentaries. A different and more restrained critique has been offered by Cardinal George Pell, reflecting church unease at the impact of a commitment to secular rights on religious preoccupations about abortion and homosexuality.

The fact that Australia is the only advanced democracy without a bill of rights forces most of these critics to take the position of Voltaire's Dr Pangloss, who believed he lived in the best of all possible worlds, and was adept at finding facile arguments to justify evils such as wars, earthquakes and torture. They claim that in Australia we live in the best of all possible constitutional worlds and we are actually governed better, or more democratically, than any other country. This tends to ramp up the 'It ain't broke, so don't fix it' argument a few notches, to, 'It's unique and wonderful, so don't fix it' – an appeal to patriotism at the expense of reality. Of course, the very fact that Australia is the only progressive country without a bill of rights enables these critics to trawl through the tens of thousands of cases decided in other countries, and select a few that seem odd. Obviously courts on occasion make wrong decisions, although the examples selected by the critics often turn out, on closer inspection, to be no example at all: some are misreported, others are quite justifiable when you consider all the facts, while several have already been exploded as urban myths in their country of origin.

Charter cynics have adopted Cardinal Pell's observation: 'It is instructive to note that Zimbabwe has a constitutional bill of rights . . . just to list these rights against the present situation in Zimbabwe shows how fragile they are.'[1] This is absolutely true, but misses the point. The reason that constitutional rights are so fragile in Zimbabwe is that Robert Mugabe has terrorised and replaced the judges: in 2001 Chief Justice Anthony Gubbay fled after receiving physical threats from 'war veteran' thugs, and was replaced by Mr Mugabe's own, obedient, attorney-general. Other High Court judges were outrageously bribed by being given farms that had been 'repossessed' from whites. There are still a few courageous magistrates – I appeared in Harare for a journalist accused of publishing 'false news' about the government, and he was acquitted by a magistrate whose car was set on fire by thugs. The journalist was, of course, deported by Mugabe after his acquittal. This simply makes the point that no bill of rights can work if the independence of the judiciary is destroyed – an unlikely prospect in Australia.

There are even better examples, my favourite being the freedom-loving Bolshevik Nikolai Bukharin, Lenin's top lieutenant. Bukharin presented his leader with a bill of rights he had drafted in an effort to ensure that their revolution did not, as the French Revolution had, degenerate into terror. Lenin waved away his 'anti-Thermidorean catechism' with the words, 'Comrade, I see no need to circulate this. It is a childish idea, that we could stop or forestall so fatal a development with a sheet of paper.' After Lenin's death Bukharin, who opposed the liquidation of the kulaks, lost the power struggle with Stalin. In 1936 he was given the task of writing the Soviet constitution, in which he duly placed his bill of rights. A year later he was arrested, and in 1938 he was dishonestly show-trialled and peremptorily shot – one of ten million victims of Stalin's terror.[2] So no one suggests that bills of rights are proof against murderous dictatorships, although they can serve as warning beacons against a slide into tyranny. They are designed to improve society and governance in stable democracies.

———

Cardinal Pell is, naturally enough, concerned about 'the fate of the right to religious liberty under a charter of rights'. Since religious liberty is guaranteed, his anxiety is misplaced. Churches are not public bodies, so they are not bound by the statute, except – under some charters – when they undertake public duties, such as running schools or nursing homes. Whether they will be so bound will require a decision by parliament when enacting the statute. (The Victorian bill of rights exempts churches – wrongly in my view – in all such respects. If churches, for their own purposes, set up institutions for the vulnerable, why should they be exempt from a duty to treat their charges with a minimum of humanity?).

Pell's concerns about Britain are largely based on an article written by a Catholic legal academic in 1980 – two decades before the Human Rights Act came into force. The only case the cardinal comes up with to dispute the value of the British act concerns a zealous pro-life campaigner, a Mrs Connelly, who sent photos of aborted foetuses to pharmacists in order to shame them out of stocking the morning-after pill.[3] She was fined for sending grossly offensive unsolicited material through the post, to the distress of recipients. Pell complains that her defence, namely her right to religious expression, was rejected by the English court, which found it was outweighed by the rights of citizens to go about their lawful business without being subjected to distress.

I can understand and even share Pell's disappointment at this decision, but it cannot be an argument *against* a bill of rights, because the campaigner had no rights at all before its enactment. She would have had to plead guilty, because without a bill she could raise no defence of freedom of speech. Properly analysed, the case shows the advantage from Pell's perspective of a charter, because it gave Mrs Connelly a defence that might have succeeded. That it failed is not an argument against a charter, but an argument for its more active enforcement.

It is surprising that nobody told the cardinal about a more important case, which actually led to a change in the law to enhance at election time the freedom of speech of anti-abortion campaigners (as well as other campaign groups such as Greenpeace and the Campaign for Nuclear Disarmament). It concerned a Mrs Bowman, as dedicated an anti-abortion campaigner as Mrs Connolly. Before the general election she printed and distributed leaflets in a number of constituencies, with pictures of foetuses on the back and the voting record on abortion issues of each candidate on the front. She was prosecuted under an old law that made it a crime for anyone other than a political party to spend more than £5 at an election to support a particular candidate. I defended her and she was acquitted on a technicality, but we still took the case to the European Court of Human Rights, which declared that her very prosecution was a breach of the right of free speech.[4] The British government was forced to change the law to allow campaigning groups to play a more involved part in elections.

Pell concludes, '*Connolly v. DPP* shows how little protection religious people can expect from anything like the UK Human Rights Act if it were to be implemented in Australia.' On the contrary, it shows that even maladroit forms of religious expression such as Mrs Connolly's will have some protection – overridden though it may be by the rights of others – and that genuine forms of political activity based on religious beliefs, like those of Mrs Bowman, will have real protection.

Christian churches must be careful and consistent in their responses to the bill of rights debate. On any view, Christ came into the world to succour the poor, the vulnerable and the despised. If that remains the Christian message, then mounting evidence that a bill of rights serves to help these very people should engage the support of Christian churches. Cardinal Pell has made no comment on this aspect of the debate. His church, which has played a notable part in Australia and aboard in the struggle for liberty of conscience, has belatedly acknowledged (largely as a result of the increasing awareness of human rights) that its own institutions have harboured a number of child abusers. Its doctrinal hostility to contraception has been criticised for contributing to deaths through the HIV virus of some of its followers and their partners in Africa. Other churches have motes in their own eyes, while extreme religions and cults have been capable of great cruelty in separating families, brainwashing converts and hating apostates.

These practices cannot be stopped by a bill of rights, unless the religious organisation supplies public services or uses public money, but a general awareness of the importance of individual liberty can assist their victims (for example, young women who seek to marry outside a sect), and educate police and community services about the need to protect them from reprisals. More positively, in times of terrorism or racial tension a bill of rights provides some comfort – psychological and legal – to insecure religious minorities, requiring government agencies to take action to protect them from serious harassment and abuse. So church leaders should think carefully before they oppose a measure that can do some good for those same vulnerable people for whom they preach the need for Christian charity.

The most marked feature of opposition to the charter has been the notion that it will prove a financial bonanza for lawyers, who therefore support it for self-interested reasons. Bob Carr has long made this the leitmotif of his campaign against human rights: 'LAWYERS ARE ALREADY DRUNK WITH POWER' is the title of his diatribe against 'elitist' lawyers intoxicated by 'the whiff of litigation'.[5] 'EXPERIENCE SUGGESTS A NATIONAL CHARTER OF RIGHTS WOULD BE A BANQUET, RATHER THAN A PICNIC, FOR LAWYERS' proclaim the editors of The Australian, and its columns are full of bile about 'fat-cat' lawyers (Paul Kelly now simply calls them 'fat' lawyers), while Janet Albrechtsen changes the metaphor to a less loveable animal: 'like pigs sniffing for truffles, lawyers can smell the enticing waft of money'.[6] This point routinely appears as a principle objection to the charter in the Australian press. When I made some pro-charter remarks in an interview with The Australian, the editors requested the journalist ask me by email the following question: 'Does Geoffrey not think he has a conflict of interest, since he is a lawyer?' My reply was that I felt no conflict at all. Most of the human rights cases I have conducted over the years have been without charge (my wife jokes that the two words she most dreads are *pro* and *bono*), except, of course, when I act for News Ltd and other media companies in efforts to protect their freedom of expression. The question calls for a more considered response.

Lawyers have always attracted obloquy, justified when they batten on to human misery, but sometimes an undeserved shot at members of a profession that has a duty to act with dedication for all – however unpleasant – who seek its services. Many lawyers live comfortably on the fees they charge, although they would probably make more as real-estate agents or merchant bankers. But what the critics fail to understand – and their ignorance in this respect is extraordinary – is the fact that there are different kinds of lawyers. Commercial lawyers earn the most money because they act for the wealthiest clients, usually corporations, and substantial fees are charged for tax or trade practices advice and other corporate services. These 'fat-cat' areas do not involve human rights and will be little affected by a charter that can be invoked only by individuals.

At the other end of the financial scale are the lawyers who are actually concerned with human rights and are likely to bring charter cases. They are no less able, but through temperament or idealism they work in public-interest law centres, or in community law offices, or legal aid, or in the Aboriginal legal service, or in trade union or NGO offices. They are on salaries, and salaries that are extremely modest, ranging from \$40,000 to \$60,000 per year – the same wage band as a cadet journalist. This is easily ascertainable, but no journalist or commentator has ever mentioned it. A recent report showed salaries for lawyers in community centres were about sixty per cent of those of lawyers doing equivalent work in the public service.[7]

So the financial awards of human rights lawyers do not compare with the emoluments of those who demonise them, or the perks of politicians, including the massive perks of former New South Wales state premiers (or the hefty salaries of newspaper editors). Yet these are the lawyers who will be principally involved in taking up charter cases, and, if necessary, litigating them. Established QCs, and young lawyers from major commercial firms, have been providing *pro bono* services to community interest law centres and proffering advice on the Victorian and ACT charters, which (as the critics never note), have not become banquets or picnics or even takeaways for lawyers, fat or slim.[18]

The venom of the attacks on lawyers in the charter debate is something of an Australian phenomenon – it has not featured much in debates over charters in other countries. It makes a false point, because many opponents of the charter are in fact lawyers, often from the wealthy end of town, who are resistant to change and are uninterested in the profession's duty to help the poor and vulnerable. The really significant fact is that lawyers who do have the relevant experience almost unanimously believe that a charter will make a difference to their work and make justice more readily attainable.

In any event, the great thing about a charter – and this development is noticeable now in Britain – is that it does not need lawyers. It is a law that, unlike most other statutes, everyone can understand. Increasingly, charter claims do not come to court or even require legal advice, because the justice of them can be recognised by the public service, when advanced by the victim, or by concerned professionals such as doctors and nurses. The great educational benefits of a charter do not involve lawyers, they involve teachers and historians, priests and politicians and public servants, and, most of all, editors and journalists who are willing to promote the cause of liberty.

———

It is a measure of the confusion surrounding the debate on an Australian bill of rights that while Bob Carr warns the ALP conference, 'The conservatives are more likely to make a charter work for them than the Labor side of politics'[9] shadow attorney-general George Brandis looks this gift-horse in the mouth by asserting that Australians have no need for a bill of rights because of 'the strength of our protection of rights and liberties'.[10] Cornelia Rau, David Hicks, Dr Haneef, Vivian Alvarez Solon and others who have experienced the strength of Australia's protection of their liberties might beg to disagree. But in August 2008 the federal liberal party decided to adopt Bob Carr's argument that it would be wrong to give any further power to an unelected judiciary, stating – with astonishing historical ignorance – that a charter 'might create a Star Chamber', which was abolished in Britain in 1641 precisely to ensure that henceforth real judges, independent of the king, would decide all legal cases.[11]

What is it about a bill of rights that makes people crusade against it? Here is Bob Carr's opening salvo in 2002:

> Parliaments are elected to make laws. In doing so, they make judgements about how the rights and interests of the public should be balanced. Views will differ in any given case about whether the judgement is correct. However, if the decision is

unacceptable, the community can make its views known at regular elections. This is our political tradition.[12]

This is not only 'our' political tradition. It is the tradition in every democratic nation. But at those elections, as Mr Carr and any other savvy politician, such as Bill Clinton, knows, 'It's the economy, stupid' will be the main issue in the campaign. The questions that most commonly come before courts under bills of rights – questions about whether decisions on individuals are unfair or discriminatory – will rarely feature in any election discussion, let alone in any parliamentary debate, and the community will not, by voting for one of two political parties, be able to pass judgement on any given case. And if during an election a promise impacting on civil liberties appears on the platform of a successful party, then that party in government will have the power to pass the law they promised the electorate, which the courts must obey, even if it restricts human rights. Where, then, is the problem? Carr goes on:

A bill of rights would make a fundamental shift in that tradition, with the parliament abdicating its important policy-making functions to the judiciary.

A statutory bill of rights would do no such thing. As we have seen, any parliament that passed it would not be abdicating policy, it would be *making* policy – a perfectly good policy: namely, that its laws should henceforth be interpreted, so far as possible, consistently with liberty. If parliament says clearly that it does not intend a particular law to be consistent with liberty, then so be it – parliament has made apparent its policy in relation to that law, and the courts must obey. It is absurd to talk of parliamentary 'abdication' of policy – on the contrary, the New South Wales parliament already has a committee that scrutinises laws for human rights defects. Is this a form of abdication? No doubt this committee would continue its work under a charter, much assisted by court decisions and occasional declarations of incompatibility, which would be referred to it. At all times parliament would retain its sovereign role as policymaker. It can be assisted by court decisions, but it remains supreme. Better informed, but supreme. How, then, can this be a 'fundamental shift' in a democratic tradition, when every other democracy, either by constitution or statute, utilises court interpretations of human rights standards to inform and improve its legislation?

Some of the scare stories Carr tells are, when scrutinised, simply wrong. Some are urban myths and others are based on inaccurate reports. Here are a few examples, taken from an article he wrote, of how Carr, I am sure unconsciously, misleads his readers.[13]

In the most recent burst of judicial activism, judges in Britain have determined that the Justice Secretary can no longer block a parole board decision to release a dangerous prisoner.

On the contrary, judges in Britain's Court of Appeal found that the Home Secretary *can* block any release by the parole board of a 'dangerous' prisoner (a prisoner whom the board finds is not dangerous, but remains dangerous in the mind of the minister) under an existing act of parliament. That act, said the Court of Appeal, was contrary to the human rights requirement that a prisoner's liberty can only be denied by the decision of an independent court or tribunal (such as the parole board), and not at the arbitrary whim of a politician. The court upheld the Home Secretary's decision because of the existing law, and could only issue a declaration of incompatibility under its bill of rights.[14] In due course, the Home Secretary's appeal succeeded in the highest court, so Carr's point turns out to be utterly wrong – the law was compatible after all! In the meantime, however, parliament has considered the point and is likely to amend the law to enable the independent parole board to make the decision on whether to release the prisoner, rather than the Home Secretary, who admitted in the course of the proceedings 'that there can be no legitimate political input into the decision'. So Carr's point is quite goofy. Politicians, as the British ministers accept, are not elected to decide the length of sentence of individual prisoners – unless they are corrupt Labor politicians such as the NSW Minister for Corrective Services, Rex Jackson, who was bribed heavily in the 1980s to do just that. Carr's example is not only wrong, but betrays a discomfort with the doctrine of the separation of powers between the executive and the judiciary – a doctrine crucial to democratic governance.

Judges also determined that failed asylum seekers

in Britain could have access to the National Health Scheme, again something that should be a matter for elected politicians.

This case had nothing to do with the Human Rights Act. Indeed, the court rejected the suggestion that the asylum seekers' rights were breached, and decided the case simply by interpreting the statute in the way parliament intended: to give failed asylum seekers who had become 'ordinarily resident' for twelve months (like the applicant) access to free medical treatment.[15] It therefore overruled the minister, who had misinterpreted the law.

Carr continues:

> In Scotland, because of a delay in placing toilets in prison cells, the Scottish *Law Reporter* estimates that prisoners may be entitled to awards totalling £76 million because their cells violated the European charter of Fundamental Rights. The government had been caught up with another priority, expanding drug rehabilitation programs for inmates.

This example actually demonstrates the value of a charter. Carr euphemistically says 'their cells violated the European charter', instead of explaining that it was incompetent Scottish Labour politicians who violated the European Convention of Human Rights, by their failure to end the disgusting Victorian-era practice of forcing prisoners to 'slop out' their chamber pots once a day. It was well known by 2001 that this practice would soon be condemned by the European

Court as amounting to ill-treatment, not only for prisoners but for prison officers, who complained that they were forced to endure the stench of human excrement whenever they entered these ancient, airless cells.[16] The Prison Officers' Association demanded reform and the Scottish parliament allocated £13 million to provide sewage facilities. The relevant minister diverted the funds to other programmes, and five years later the first prisoner who sued was awarded £2450 in damages. That was in 2004. Still the ministry did not heed the warning, and four years later the law lords permitted other prisoners – and prison officers – to claim compensation for what on any view was a case of government maladministration. It was not merely a 'delay in placing toilets in prison cells'. It was a series of cock-ups by a government that deliberately consigned prison officers and their prisoners to an unhealthy and degrading environment, knowing, or else not caring, about the legal consequences. A good example, one might think, of how a bill of rights serves to galvanise ministers and public servants, and as a last resort to hold them to account when they fail to take the action that is required in the public interest.

Last year £750,000 was paid to 197 heroin addicted prisoners who successfully argued that cutting short their treatment while in prison breached their human rights.

Once again, misinformation about British case law is being passed on to Australians. The heroin addicts did not argue successfully – indeed, they did not argue at all, because their case was settled out of court. The reason that the government settled had nothing to do with the Human Rights Act, but with the fact it had seriously injured these prisoners by first placing them on methadone and then inappropriately and negligently subjecting them to 'cold turkey' detoxification. This mistaken policy, which came from trying to use prison as a treatment centre for drug addicts, was carelessly operated, and the prisoners who sued would in any event have won damages for negligence, without any reliance on human rights claims. So the government had to settle and paid a modest £3500 to compensate each injured prisoner.

> But there's another phenomenon that perverts proper process: police and bureaucrats in Britain anticipate getting overruled on human rights grounds and start to shape their responses. Pity the factory owner who, this month, had to pay £20,000 to bailiffs to remove 40 gypsies who had torn down a 2.4m fence and occupied his factory land. The police refused to act so as not to breach the travellers' human rights.

This appears to be one of the stories about gypsies that the British parliamentary committee described recently as 'urban myths'. In March 2006 the highest court ruled that eviction of gypsies did *not* breach their human rights. Parliament has legislated to give police extra powers to remove travellers and trespassers from private land and these have never been challenged under the Human Rights Act. Police are sometimes reluctant to use them unless there is a breach of the peace: their decisions not to evict gypsies have nothing to do with human rights, but have been made by a number of forces because of manpower shortages. That is why private landowners have had to resort to bailiffs.

Bob Carr's latest furphy – part of his internal Labor party scare campaign – is to suggest that a future conservative government might add a 'right of property' to the charter, which conservative judges might then decide would be breached by 'green initiatives' that Labor governments may want to pass. This argument, which seems to have persuaded Young Labor to oppose the charter, is obviously wrong.[17] The right to property is the one right already protected in the federal constitution: private property cannot be acquired by government except on just terms. It is, of course, already fully protected by statute and common law (see the law of theft) and it is difficult to think of any Australian government that would try to seize someone's property without compensation, unless it was suspected of being stolen property. Any federal law that did so could never pass muster under Section 51 of the constitution, irrespective of any bill of rights. If parliament wants to undertake a 'green initiative' by controlling the clearance of native vegetation (Carr's particular example), then parliament can do so: individuals have no right to use their land free from planning controls that serve the best interests of the community.

I am diffident about criticising Bob Carr: I have known him since his days as an industrial roundsman on *The Bulletin*, and when he was premier I acted for him (free of charge, I hasten to add) in a grand plan to exhume Governor Phillip from his obscure grave and bring him back in honour to the city he founded (a plan scuppered by the Church of England, which has lost his body).[18] But his campaign to deny his fellow citizens a right to fair and humane treatment seems to have scared politicians in both major parties. What really frightens them is the regrettable fact that any government that brings in a bill of rights in Australia will be subject to ill-informed criticism, especially if the introduction has been contested by the opposition.

When a court decision displeases the media, they usually look for someone or something to blame. There is a danger that the press will blame the bill of rights (A BILL OF WRONGS!) for any decision in favour of unpopular people such as prisoners and asylum seekers, although very often the same decision would have been reached without one. (Victorian Attorney-General Rob Hulls was abused in the media because Tony Mokbel's lawyers invoked the Victorian charter on behalf of this much-vilified gangland murder suspect – there was little publicity subsequently when his claim was rejected). It is a favourite tactic of the 'whinging comms' to denounce the charter whenever it is invoked by an unpopular defendant in a hopeless cause: they fail to realise that bad points can be taken by litigants without the help of a charter, and courts quickly reject them or strike them out (usually with costs immediately awarded against the presumptuous litigant), under their power to reject claims that are hopeless or frivolous or vexatious.

It is easy for opponents to caricature, or to misrepresent, the way in which a statutory bill of rights works, so any government that introduces the charter must display a certain amount of political courage. For this reason, Carr's appeal is really to the political cowardice of his Labor colleagues – it is certainly not an appeal to statesmanship. If the evidence shows that a bill of rights works in favour of citizens in a democracy – and it does – then politicians who shrink from supporting it betray the trust of those who elect them in the belief that they will act to advance the public interest.

—

The Australian newspaper crusades against a charter, so let us look at its arguments in an October 2008 editorial. 'It is a mistake to freeze rights and consign them to judges.'[19] But a right is not a 'right' unless it can be enforced. Enforcement is by law – by order of judges. So unless rights are consigned to judges, they cannot be enforced and are not rights. And rights are not 'frozen' in a statutory bill: they are universal principles to which parliament can add (for example, disability rights), and courts can explicate and apply to new situations.

The editorial states: 'Even a statutory bill of rights shifts the balance of power towards an unelected judiciary.' No, it doesn't – because, as I have explained, parliament reigns supreme and can repeal the charter when ever it likes. By enacting a charter it signals its intention to have its laws interpreted consistently with human rights. This is the intention of most decent MPs, and is the intention that will be implemented by the judiciary. And when will journalists understand that judges are unelected precisely so that they are independent of politics and can deploy their learning about what fairness requires without fear or political favour?

'It encourages atrophy in the organs of democracy.' This is an bizarre charge. A statutory bill of rights requires the establishment of a parliamentary committee to check legislation for consistency; it encourages debate on whether legislation is consistent; and it requires further debates in those cases where legislation proves to be inconsistent. It makes 'the organs of democracy' – cabinet and public service, legislature and the judiciary – more conscious of the need to respect the human rights of citizens, and more active in doing so. The evidence from the ACT and Victoria already shows that the organs of democracy are much less lethargic, as committees and parliaments debate issues in legislation spot-lit by their charters.

It may be that the editors of *The Australian* have become confused by reading their own newspaper. In its comment pages, hardly a week goes by without Janet Albrechtsen or James Allan attacking bills of rights and those who support them. Albrechtsen sees them as a left-wing plot – 'a leftoid [sic] symbol of disdain for the people's choices'. Her articles alternate abuse with apoplectic predictions drawn from Cold War hyperbole: 'A new war on democracy is taking hold across the west. It's been launched by activist judges trying to overturn the will of the people.'[20] These 'hoons' have 'plotted out a stealth strategy aimed at duping us into believing a charter is harmless'.[21] The judges in her Spielberg horror scenario 'armed with a charter to hijack government policy' are 'high octane law-makers', a 'galloping imperial judiciary' who dismount to write 'judicial graffiti'.[22] Ms Albrechtsen's prose is so purple it's practically puce, but when she recovers from her own mixed metaphors – one moment it's high octane judicial tanks on her lawn, the next it's hoon judges besieging her mind, the next she's being attacked by the galloping judicial cavalry – her message is simplistic: 'You may disagree with some government policies, but at least you can boot out politicians when they get things wrong.' No, you can't – not for three or four years, and then for reasons that relate to the economy, not to human rights. You can't boot them out because the public service has denied your child a place at school, or has sent your private details to commercial marketers, or has refused your partner a benefit he or she deserves. Who cares, when MPs don't? A charter gives the courts adequate power to protect individuals from government and public service abuses. That is their role in a democracy.

James Allan is a self-proclaimed refugee from Canada – a place, he tells us, where judges are driven mad by regular contact with a charter of rights. Allan has assimilated well here, with a professorship at the University of Queensland, although he still cannot understand our 'bizarre practice of acknowledging the traditional owners of the land'.[23] He is the author of such articles as 'DON'T GIVE JUDGES MORE POWER'; 'POLLIES OR JUDGES TO RULE THE ROOST?'; 'GIVING

Lawyers More Power Will Cut Our Liberties'; 'Mad Game to Tinker with Our Great System'; 'Political Correctness Stifles Debate'; 'Balancing Competing Rights Requires Trade-offs'; 'Why a Bill of Rights is Wrong'; 'Human Rights Approach to Immigration Muddleheaded, Wrong and Dangerous'; 'Hulls Glosses over Inconvenient Truths' and so on – and on and on.[24] Mr Allan is also a Panglossian ('Our system is better than the systems in the US, Canada, Britain and New Zealand'), a believer that Australians live in the best of all possible constitutional worlds compared with his native Canada, to which he annually returns to fish for more horror stories about the behaviour of its power-crazed jurists. He does not explain why, if the governance of his native country is so unhinged as a result of its charter, it has not been repealed, or indeed why his countrymen and women were so pleased with it when it was a mere statute that they allowed their representatives to upgrade it to a constitutional provision. Why, if government policy has been so damaged by the charter, is its governance still good enough for Canada to beat Australia to a place in the G7?

Mr Allan's objections tend to be summed up in sound bites: 'Judges will win; elected legislators will lose'.[25] He demonises Australian judges by describing them as 'aristo-crats' or members of a 'juristocrisy', who are hell-bent on 'ruling the roost'.[26] In so doing he hopes, no doubt, to play on his adopted country's egalitarian instincts. Should his suggestion that they are power-hungry aristocrats be doubted (perhaps by some reader who actually knows a judge) he reaches for the all-time greatest insult – they're not judges or juristocrats, they are, wait for it, 'a group of ex-lawyers'.[27] This is literally true but, of course, disguises the real point that they are ex-lawyers who have been appointed as judges because of their moral character, integrity and legal knowledge. Moreover, they are 'ex' in the sense that they are independent, they no longer have clients or causes, and can adjudicate disputes and grievances impartially – more impartially, in particular, than politicians or pundits.

What is depressing about the Australian debate – or at least the debate in *The Australian* – over the charter is how it concentrates on the assumed defects of 'unelected judges'. There is rarely any recognition to the way a charter encourages parliament into enlivening and engaging debate on human rights issues. There is never any reference to its value as a 'mind how you go' for public servants or to how, after ten years in Britain, there is mounting evidence of its use by public interest groups to improve the lots of vulnerable people without the need to go to court or to involve lawyers, let alone judges. These dimensions – in some respects the most important consequences of a charter – are never mentioned in editorials on the subject.

—

Are there other, or better, arguments to be made against a charter? It is said, with some force, that its language is vague, and may tend to uncertainty. This ignores the fact that much of the common law, and a lot of statutory language, is couched in general words, and it has always been the judge's function to narrow the language appropriately for each concrete case. The concept of 'reasonableness' is a good example – it runs right through our administrative law and allows judges the scope to deliver justice by deciding what is reasonable in a particular set of circumstances.

Moreover, it is not as though Australian judges will be applying these standards in a vacuum – we have our own precedents and can utilise the work of our academics. But judges can also draw on the case law of top courts in other countries. Who would not want them to make use of jurisprudence from the US Supreme Court, or of important decisions from the South African constitutional court, or the respected work of judges in Britain? More importantly, our courts can give back a charter jurisprudence of their own, so Australians can contribute to the ongoing march of human rights with the work of our own distinguished jurists on issues such as the definition of torture, the limits of the right to privacy, the question of what new forms of bondage amount to slavery, and so on. We should show the same sort of pride in our jurisprudential accomplishments as we have in the international achievements of our scientists and sports people, our literary figures and creative artists – a pride at our ability to contribute to the development of human rights throughout the world.

A more weighty objection is whether our judges are up to it. Critics have a point when they describe the bench at present as predominantly male, middle-minded and middle-class, largely drawn from commercial law practices and with a social outlook that seems quite conservative. Might they lack sympathy with the idea of human rights, and either ignore them or interpret them in a reactionary way? The answer is that any force in this objection will soon fade, because judges are trained to apply the spirit of the law they are provided with. If parliament passes a statute of liberty, they will follow it with increasing fidelity, whatever their private reservations. That is their discipline: they are constrained by the prospects of appeal to a higher court and by the very openness of their reasoning, which will be subject to critiques by colleagues, by academics and by the public. Initially, their decisions may disappoint, but they will hardly do damage. And if they do, parliament can always reverse their interpretation by legislation. The experience of other countries is that the judiciary begins cautiously, but within a few years develops an approach that accords with the spirit of the charter. This movement is assisted by a process in which university law schools will teach it, the legal profession will absorb it and the legal culture will gradually change as legal education and professional literature will be based on fresh assumptions.

How does having a charter improve the quality of judging? For a start, it encourages judges – and those who read their work – to go back into history to understand the purpose and extent of the liberty at issue. Usually, the quality of their prose improves. They write with more clarity, in a way that readers are capable of understanding – not just lawyers but (thanks to the fact that they now must talk in charter principles rather than via detailed case law), a wider public. Because a charter sets out the governing principles, there is no need for the current self-indulgence of spending tens of thousands of words reciting the facts and discussing the merits of old cases: judgements will be much shorter, more logical and more comprehensible. Book-length High Court decisions will be consigned to the past and Australians will at last be able to understand their own law.

Another objection to a bill of rights, credible at first blush but on examination misplaced, is that it helps to foster a 'compensation culture', in which those who have suffered some trivial setback at the hands of the authorities will rush to lawyers in the hope of obtaining damages, rather than suffer, as previously, in silence. This criticism might apply to the common law of negligence, which in Australia is in a state of some uncertainty over the extent to which local authorities can be made liable for unforeseen injury. But the Human Rights Act will only compensate (and quite modestly) for real pain that has been carelessly or callously inflicted in breach of a civil right. (Less serious acts of humiliation may well be stopped without the cases being taken to court, or else without compensation.)

Take the English case where a severely disabled woman with six children was housed by her local council in a property where she could not use her wheelchair, could not therefore look after the children, and did not have access to a toilet or washing facility. The council kept her in these intolerable conditions for two years. The High Court held that her right to privacy and family life had been breached, and her 'physical and psychological integrity' had been damaged by a callous bureaucracy. The case is an example of how the act can help vulnerable and disempowered law-abiding citizens. She received modest compensation (£10,000) for her two years of humiliation, and the judge explained:

Concerns have been expressed in various quarters about the development of a 'compensation culture'. In my experience in this court, dealing with a wide range of complaints about public authorities, most citizens who have suffered as a result of some bureaucratic error are not motivated, or at least not primarily motivated, by a desire for monetary compensation. They institute proceedings because they feel outraged by what they see as an injustice and want 'them,' the faceless persons in an apparently insensitive, unresponsive and impenetrable bureaucratic labyrinth, to acknowledge that something has gone wrong, to provide them with an explanation, an apology and an assurance that steps have been taken to ensure (so far as possible in an imperfect world) that the same mistake will not happen again. This assurance will at least give them the satisfaction of knowing that they have not suffered in vain.[28]

In situations like this, where decent Australian citizens have been treated uncaringly or uncivilly by agencies of the state, do we really want to deny them any remedy, and deny society the best deterrent to others who might suffer such treatment? The critics who talk acidly about 'unelected judges' and 'fat-cat lawyers' apparently do, although few seem to have had any experience of fighting for the poor and oppressed. Maybe the view from editorial boardrooms is that people who get into trouble with officialdom have only themselves to blame. The public, I suspect, feels differently.

A charter has many uses that its critics do not dispute or mention. Although their rhetoric focuses on the threat to democracy of unelected judges, their argument has a touching naivety in assuming that MPs and journalists between them can somehow right all wrongs. Trial by newspaper is all very well, but trial by judge is better. Moreover, the critics relegate the citizens' role in democratic governance to voting meekly in elections every few years, without having the power to challenge inhumane or unfair government decisions against them by going to court. This is the only 'power' that a charter bestows. It does not take this power away from elected governments (who obviously do not need it), or shift it to unelected judges (who simply make decisions for or against litigants): it bestows this power for the first time on citizens. That is why a charter of liberty, properly analysed, gives a new power to the people – an eminently democratic thing to do.

8

The Statute
of Liberty

If the Australian parliament were minded to pass a
statute of liberty, there would have to be cross-party
agreement on its contents. The UK was fortunate in
this regard: the European Convention was there for the
taking, drafted by British lawyers using the template of
the Universal Declaration of Human Rights. South Africa
went through a longer process, drawing upon its own
struggle with apartheid. The Victorian and ACT charters
were modelled on the British statute, but the Western
Australian inquiry suggested the inclusion of economic and
social rights, and opted for a lengthy, but straightforward,
preamble. Although it is trite to say of other good ideas that
the devil is in the detail, it is not difficult to identify and
describe the universal minimum rights that are guaranteed
by all international conventions, in more or less the same
terminology. The interesting part comes in deciding
whether to add social or environmental rights, or rights

that have recently emerged. The even more interesting question is whether they should be garnished with an Australian flavour, at least within the preamble.

As John Howard discovered, it is not easy to draft preambles. Notwithstanding help from poet Les Murray, his constitutional effort for the 1999 referendum on the republic was considered stumblebum: 'We value excellence as well as fairness, independence as dearly as mateship.' Drafting by committee may not be much better. An advisory committee on the constitution in 1986 produced the following, despite Tom Keneally's help:

> **Whereas** the people are drawn from a rich diversity of cultures yet are one in their devotion to the Australian traditions of equality, the freedom of the person and the dignity of the individual;

> **Whereas** the Australian people look to share fairly in the plenty of our Commonwealth;

> **Whereas** Australia is a continent of immense extent and unique in the world, demanding as our homeland our respect, devotion and wise management.

'Whereas' this and 'whereas' are legalistic to a fault, and it is over-optimistic to suggest that the country has 'plenty' and we are all content with a share that is only 'fair'. The lines are also plodding – why should 'immense extent' demand 'respect'?

But it is easy to criticise, and I hope readers will themselves critique my wet-Sunday-afternoon effort below. The greatest constitutional preamble began in Thomas Jefferson's first draft: 'We hold these truths to be sacred and undeniable'. When he read it to Benjamin Franklin, the latter shook his head, responding: 'Smacks of the pulpit, Mr Jefferson, smacks of the pulpit. They are . . . self-evident, are they not?' Jefferson had to agree and the rest is history – US history, anyway'.[1]

Australian history should feature prominently in our preamble. Acts of parliament normally have a short title, and 'An Act to Make Better Provision for Liberty in Australia' would make the point that the charter provisions are to be generously and progressively interpreted.

A statute of liberty might look like this. I am not suggesting my text is in any way definitive, except when it reproduces the Universal Declaration. It simply gives the flavour of a charter that would provide Australia with the most advanced human rights standards in the world. If we are, as a nation, to have a charter, why not opt for the best?

AN ACT TO DECLARE THE RIGHTS AND FREEDOMS OF THE PEOPLE AND TO MAKE BETTER PROVISION FOR LIBERTY IN AUSTRALIA

Parliament,

Conscious of its democratic duty to uphold, protect and advance the hard-won liberties of the Australian people, united in one indissoluble Commonwealth;

Humble in acknowledging the first owners and occupiers

of this unique continent; whose ancestors have walked about on its earth for many thousands of years before British settlement;

Sorrowful for the dispossession, discrimination and degradation they have endured and **resolved** hereafter to respect their relationship with the land and to atone for past wrongs by future equity;

Proud nonetheless of our progress from penal colony to a free nation of boundless opportunity, unrestricted by divisions of class or caste or private wealth, and an example to the world of the ever-present possibility of reformation of the human spirit;

Dedicated to democracy as defined in the federal constitution, under which all who have a stake in the nation shall have a say in its governance;

Grateful for the British legacy of liberty first planted in this country by Governor Arthur Phillip, for Magna Carta's great promise that to no one will justice be denied or delayed, for jury trial and the importance of free speech, for a common law that presumes innocence and abominates torture and for the way these fundamental freedoms have been nurtured and embellished by generations of Australians;

Cognisant of the achievements of our country in providing better ways of working through labour rights and collective bargaining and the basic wage;

Mindful that rights entail responsibilities, and that Australia expects its people to show tolerance, respect and mutual consideration for their fellows, to abjure violence and embrace peaceful change, and willingly to share community burdens for the common good of the Commonwealth;

Determined that all shall have a stake in the prosperity of this nation and those most in need shall have a moral and legal claim on our compassion;

Inspired by the Anzac tradition of preparedness to fight for freedom, internationally and in our region, against any movement that threatens to extinguish the rights of humankind;

Respectful of the Universal Declaration of Human Rights, in the drafting of which Australia had the privilege to participate, and of all the treaties we have ratified to uphold the dignity of individuals in this nation and throughout the world;

Resolved that the liberties our forbears struggled and sacrificed to achieve shall hereafter inure to the benefit of all who live in this land,

Hereby declares that in order to advance a fair Australia, the liberties set forth in this charter shall be protected in the manner hereinafter provided.

CHARTER OF AUSTRALIAN LIBERTY

1. FREEDOM FROM SLAVERY

That there can be no slavery in a free land and hence no slaves.
Arthur Phillip's drafting may sound odd today, but these are his words and we should make his first law the first law of liberty in the nation that he alone, in 1788, believed would come to pass.

2. PROHIBITION ON TORTURE

No one shall be subjected (a) to torture or (b) to cruel or inhumane or degrading treatment or punishment.
This is the simple and absolute principle laid down by the Universal Declaration.

3. RIGHT TO LIFE

Every person has, after he or she is born, the right to life. Any loss of life attributable to agencies of the state must be fully and independently investigated. No death penalty shall be carried out in this nation.
Liberty is properly called a 'birthright'. All questions relating to abortion and euthanasia should be left to parliament. The second sentence spells out the important corollary of the right, namely that its extinction, whether intentionally or through negligence, by police or army or paramilitary force linked in any way to government must be rigorously investigated.

4. FREEDOM FROM COMPULSION

No one shall be compelled to work except by order of a court. There shall be no conscription for military service other than in a national emergency and following approval by referendum, and in that event with provision for conscientious objection. No one should be subjected to medical or scientific experimentation unless they give their free and informed consent.

This right went into the Universal Declaration as a result of horror at the Holocaust and iniquities of the concentration camps such as forced labour and medical experimentation. It does not, of course, prevent a court from ordering community service or similar punishment. As a universal right, most treaties exempt compulsory military service, but in the light of the history of conscription in Australia, this exemption should be very narrow.

5. RIGHT TO BE SET AT LIBERTY

No one shall be detained or imprisoned other than in compliance with the law and every detained person shall have the right to bring an action for habeas corpus, namely to be produced speedily before a court and to be set free unless the detaining authority can prove its actions are lawful.

Habeas corpus is such an important and historic right that it deserves to be explained and highlighted.

6. RIGHTS ON ARREST

No one shall be arrested or imprisoned for debt or for inability to perform a contractual obligation. Persons arrested or detained on a criminal charge:

i) *shall be informed promptly and if practicable in a language they understand, of the reason for their arrest and the details of any charge;*

ii) *must be brought before a court as soon as practicable and in any event within forty-eight hours of arrest. In terrorist cases, parliament may provide for up to seven days' detention, renewable by judicial order for a further seven days.*

iii) *shall be entitled to legal advice while in custody prior to their first court appearance;*

iv) *shall be entitled to have any interviews with police or persons in authority recorded by electronic means or by an independent third party;*

v) *shall be entitled to apply to the court for bail, which if granted on security or by surety shall not be an excessive amount.*

This is a standard statement of the basic right of suspects. The first provision is there because of the concern shown by Charles Dickens, who exposed the evils of the debtors' prison, which disfigured English justice for centuries. Forty-eight hours is considered the reasonable maximum for suspects to be held in police cells, except in terrorist cases, where police may apply for an extension of custody time limits. The provision against excessive bail is found in the bill of rights of 1689. The presence of lawyers and the need to record interviews and confessions are essential safeguards against miscarriages of justice.

7. THE OPEN JUSTICE PRINCIPLE

Every court in the land shall be open to the media and the public, unless it be established beyond reasonable doubt that justice cannot be done other than by their exclusion for part of the proceedings. In any such case, the judgement of the court shall be delivered in public.

The explosion in the number of 'suppression orders' in Australia draws attention to the need for the open justice principle to be stated as a separate right. There will always be cases, for example about confidential patents or the custody of children, or when judges hear arguments about the admissibility of evidence that might prejudice jury trial, where it will be necessary to impose reporting restrictions, which should be limited to what is necessary to achieve justice for the parties.

8. RIGHT TO TRIAL BY JURY

Every person charged with an offence carrying a maximum sentence of more than one year's imprisonment has a right (which may be waived) to be tried by a jury.

The importance of this right to Australia, both in saving many convicts from the gallows and in becoming the symbol for the emancipist struggle for the rights of free settlers, has been explained in earlier chapters. Since deceptive drafting denuded the constitution of this right, it should feature prominently in the charter. At the same time, if a defendant fears a jury will be prejudiced against him (say as a result of hostile publicity), he should be entitled to waive his right and instead take his trial before three judges.

9. THE RIGHT TO FAIR TRIAL

i) *In the determination of civil rights and obligations or of any criminal charge every litigant or defendant is entitled to a fair and public hearing within a reasonable time by an independent and impartial tribunal established by law.*

ii) *Everyone charged with a criminal offence shall be presumed innocent until proved guilty according to law.*

iii) *Everyone charged with a criminal offence has the following minimum rights:*

    a) *to be informed promptly, in a language that he understands and in reasonable detail of the nature and cause of the accusation against him;*

    b) *to have adequate time and facilities for the preparation of his defence and to communicate with legal representatives;*

    c) *to attend his own trial and defend himself in person or through legal assistance of his own choosing or, if he has not sufficient means to pay for legal assistance, to be given it free when the interests of justice so require;*

    d) *to examine or have examined witnesses against him and to obtain the attendance and examination of witnesses on his behalf under the same conditions as witnesses against him;*

    e) *to have the free assistance of an interpreter if he cannot understand or speak the language used in court;*

    f) *to remain silent and to put the prosecution to proof of guilt;*

g) *if convicted, to have the right to ask a higher court for*
leave to appeal against conviction and or sentence.

This is what delivers 'justice': a fair hearing within a reasonable time by an independent and impartial court. Each of these words is freighted with meaning: there are hundreds of decisions about them going back centuries. But the words themselves are stark and simple and need no scholarly exposition. The presumption of innocence serves as a warning against 'trial by media' and puts the burden of proving guilt on those who allege it – the prosecutors. These minimum rights have been found, over the years, to be the best safeguards against miscarriages of justice: they give defendants a fair opportunity to have their case put across to the jury in the adversary system.

10. NO PUNISHMENT WITHOUT LAW

i) *No one shall be found guilty of any crime on account*
of any act or omission that did not constitute a criminal
offence under Australian or international law at the
time it was committed. Nor shall a heavier penalty be
imposed than the one that was applicable at the time
the offence was committed.

ii) *No person may be punished more than once for the*
same offence.

This is straightforward, old-fashioned fairness, of a kind that headline-grabbing politicians are apt to overlook. Under the rule of law, everything is permitted which is not specifically prohibited. Conduct may be very unpleasant or immoral, but if it is not a crime at the time it cannot be punished with hindsight. Retroactive legislation is unlawful. The government cannot keep people in prison after they have served the full sentence handed down by the court.

11. FREEDOM OF MOVEMENT

i)   *Every person lawfully present in Australia has freedom to move across state borders and to choose where in the country to live. Every holder of an Australian passport shall be entitled, subject to any court order, to leave the country, and if an Australian citizen he or she shall have the right to an Australian passport and shall be guaranteed the right to return. Every person accepted for residence in Australia shall be afforded the opportunity to become an Australian citizen.*

ii) *Australia will entertain asylum claims from any persons who come to or within its boundaries and allege they are refugees under the Refugee Convention 1951 and can establish they are fleeing from a country where they are, or have a well-founded fear of being, persecuted in a way that will endanger their life or that of family members. A precondition of such claim must be a positive wish to accept the rights and the responsibilities set forth in this charter.*

iii) *No person shall be accepted for naturalisation or citizenship unless he or she can demonstrate an understanding of this charter and can swear that they accept its responsibilities and its rights.*

Let us have no more nonsense like the Burchett Affair, where a 'liberal' government refused an Australian journalist the right to return home on the pretext that he did not have an Australian passport – he had lost it – but really because he had been a communist. Citizens of Australia have a right to return to Australia, no matter what they get up to overseas. But why should Australia tolerate intolerant people, in the sense of accepting as refugees or citizens anyone who does not believe in the liberal democratic ideals set out in this charter? If they hold beliefs that require honour killings, or death for apostates, or clitoridectomies for their daughters, let them apply elsewhere.

12. FREEDOM OF EXPRESSION AND THE RIGHT TO KNOW

i) *Everyone has the right to freedom of expression, which includes the right to hold and express opinions, and to receive and impart information and ideas without interference by government.*

ii) *Practitioners of journalism shall have a right to protect their sources, subject only to overriding considerations of public interest.*

iii) *The above rights shall be accorded especial importance in any civil court proceedings in which they are properly invoked.*

iv) *This right shall create a presumption in favour of publication, rebuttable only if the restriction sought to be placed upon it is necessary in the interests of a democratic society to guard against incitement to crime or disorder, or to safeguard national security, or to enable other citizens to stop lies being told about them, or to preserve confidential information or to protect their privacy as defined in Article 13.*

v) *Citizens have a right to know about the workings of their government. In addition to their rights under the Freedom of Information Act, and subject to iv) above, all cabinet papers and other government documents shall be made available for public inspection within ten years of their creation.*

vi) *These rights may be invoked by media corporations on behalf of their journalists and editors, and/or on behalf of their readers, viewers or listeners.*

I have opted, with regret, for the European rather than the American approach. I have found too many Australians are afraid of full-blooded free speech of the kind permitted to Americans under their First Amendment, who may say what they like about public figures, provided they do not make allegations recklessly or in the knowledge that they are false. The British and European position makes a presumption that speech and writing should be unrestricted, and so requires would-be censors to prove the case for suppression in a liberal democracy. (In libel cases, for example, plaintiffs would have to prove that a statement was false in order to obtain damages for it, rather than require the media defendant to prove its statement true.) The government would have no difficulty demonstrating the need to ban race hate material or child pornography.

Sub-clause (v) is intended to abolish the absurd 'thirty-year' rule, inherited unthinkingly from British practice, under which citizens may only learn what their government has been doing thirty years after they have done it.

Thus, cabinet papers released in January 2009 revealed hitherto unknown details of what the Fraser government was really up to in 1979. There is no confidentiality justification in keeping important historical papers secret for more than ten years.

13. RIGHT TO PRIVACY
Everyone has the right to have his or her home and stable family life respected and to prevent passing on, or publication of, intimate personal details, or disclosure of personal matters concerning children in their care. Public authorities shall not interfere with the exercise of this right unless such interference serves the public interest and is in accordance with legally prescribed data-protection principles or ethics codes promulgated for the media by representative or statutory bodies.

This privacy right is limited to the protection of home, family and intimate personal details: it does not stop police obtaining a warrant to search bank accounts in appropriate cases, nor does it stop newspapers from investigatory public interest stories. Privacy can be invaded, but only in cases where such interference is necessary and proportionate – a 'mind how you go' warning to authorities that they should resist the temptation to pry, and should comply with data protection principles when storing information. In making privacy decisions that affect the media, courts are required to take into account ethics codes propagated by the media itself – for example by the Australian Press Council.

I have, doubtless to the horror of some human rights advocates, added 'stable' to the definition of family life, to exclude cases where, for example, serious criminals or illegal immigrants resist deportation on the basis of a flimsy or hasty marriage, or a family arrangement unlikely to survive if it secures their right to remain.

14. FREEDOM OF THOUGHT, CONSCIENCE AND RELIGION

Everyone has the right to freedom of thought, conscience and religion; this right includes freedom to change religion or belief, and freedom, either alone or in community with others, to manifest religion or belief in worship or other forms of observance and to expound the tenets of that religion to others. This freedom shall not extend to religions or other movements that preach hatred or incite violence and shall not protect religions from criticism made by persons exercising their free speech rights under Article 12.

Freedom of religion is freedom to worship peacefully and to proselytise, but not to vilify non-believers or punish apostates, or break up families. Religions whose preachers incite hatred obviously have no protection – and that includes hatred of women or gays, as well as hatred of Jews or Americans.

15. RIGHT TO OWN PROPERTY

i) *Everyone has the right to own property alone as well as in association with others.*

ii) *Nobody shall be deprived of his or her property arbitrarily.*

iii) *There shall be no confiscation of private property by the state other than when it is in satisfaction of a judgement*

> *debt or if it is reasonably suspected to be the proceeds of crime.*
>
> iv) *The state may acquire private property but only upon just terms.*

The right to own property is guaranteed by Article 17 of the Universal Declaration. The state may confiscate private property by law – for example in satisfaction of unpaid taxes, or if it has been bought by money obtained through crime. But it may only nationalise it in the public interest, which would include acquisition for roads or airports, or to return it to Indigenous inhabitants, or to preserve its environmental value. In all such cases of compulsory purchase, the state is required to provide 'just terms' – defined by international law as compensation that is 'prompt, adequate and effective', reflecting full market value at the moment of dispossession, plus interest to the day of payment.[2]

16. RIGHT TO WORK

i) *Everyone has the right to work, to free choice of employment, to safe and healthy conditions of work and to protection against unemployment.*

ii) *Everyone, without any discrimination, has the right to equal pay for equal work.*

iii) *Everyone who works has the right to fair remuneration, ensuring for himself and his family an existence worthy of human dignity, and supplemented, if necessary, by other means of social protection.*

iv) *Everyone has the right to form and join trade unions for the protection of their interests and in the course of that protection to have trade unions represent them in collective bargaining.*

v) *Everyone has the right to rest and leisure, including reasonable limitation of working hours and periodic holidays with pay.*

This right is basically an amalgam of Articles 23 and 24 of the Universal Declaration. I have added to (iv) its necessary implication, namely that the right to join trade unions means a right to have those trade unions represent their members in collective bargaining. This was overlooked in the ill-fated Work Choices legislation, which breached conventions of the International Labour Organisation to which Australia was party.

17. RIGHT TO WELLBEING

i) *Everyone has the right to a standard of living adequate for their health and wellbeing, including food, clothing, housing and medical care, and necessary social services and the right to security in the event of unemployment, sickness, disability, old age or other lack of livelihood in circumstances beyond their control.*

ii) *The government is required to take reasonable legislative and other measures, within its available resources, to achieve the progressive realisation of the rights in (i) above.*

iii) *Everyone has the right to due respect when treated in any hospital or nursing home or care centre or medical surgery, and where practicable to give informed consent before undergoing any invasive surgical procedure.*

This article reflects Article 25.1 of the Universal Declaration – a right that the Australian delegation at the UN in 1948 took special care to support, despite the doubts of the Americans (who still do not have a properly functioning health-care system). In (ii) I have adopted the South Africa formula sensibly applied by its constitutional court, to the effect that the government's duty is to realise these rights gradually, within its available budget.

18. RIGHT TO EDUCATION

i) *Everyone has the right to education. Education shall be free and compulsory, at least at primary and until an intermediate secondary level. Technical and professional education shall be open to all, and higher education shall be equally accessible on the basis of merit.*

ii) *The government is required to take reasonable measures, within its available resources, to make technical and professional education and higher education progressively available and affordable.*

iii) *Education shall be directed to the full development of the human personality and to the strengthening of respect for human rights and fundamental freedoms. It shall promote understanding, tolerance and the values that are set out in this charter, and shall include teaching about the history of these rights. Such teaching shall include objective accounts of the history of Australian Aborigines and Torres Strait Islanders, of their dispersion and degradation during the colonial period, and of the Stolen Generation.*

iv) *Parents have a right to choose the kind of education that shall be given to their children, subject to the right of*

> *the government to set curricula and to refuse approval to*
> *schools where teaching is or is likely to breach (iii) above.*

This article reflects Article 26 of the Universal Declaration, with some amendments necessary to ensure that the right to choose a non-secular school should be qualified to enable the state to set a core curriculum and to prohibit the teaching of intolerance. Sub-section (iii) is of particular importance: it requires human rights education in all schools. Education must not skate over this nation's own failures in respect of our Indigenous people: the racist policies and events for which we have at least, and at last, said sorry. We must not emulate countries such as Japan, where school textbooks avoid all reference to its barbaric nationalism in the Second World War. It is a measure of the maturity of a society that it can face up to the atrocities in its past – Spain, for example, is only now prepared to exhume the mass graves of Franco's death-squads and to review its own fascist record. Honesty is the best policy for teaching children well.

19. THE RIGHT TO DEMOCRACY
Every citizen and/or resident and/or taxpayer over the age
of eighteen has the right and must have the opportunity,
without discrimination:

i)   *to take part in the government in Australia, directly by*
standing for parliament or by voting, freely and secretly,
for chosen representatives;

ii)   *to have access, on terms of equality and merit, to the*
public service and to all public offices, including the
office of head of state in any Australian republic.

This is the right to democracy. Australia is unique in having a federal law that makes voting compulsory, in over-broad terms that led to a jail sentence for Albert Langer, who did no more than to encourage citizens to lodge informal votes as a protest against all political parties. (Langer was made Amnesty International's first Australian 'prisoner of conscience'.) Extending the franchise and the right to stand for parliament to certain persons who have not taken out citizenship may be controversial, but if they are residents or taxpayers they do have a stake in the country, and in the case of politicians the talent pool should be as deep as possible. As for the office of head of state, I do not see why any Australian should be debarred from aspiring to it or standing in an election for it, once a republic has been established.

20. RIGHTS OF PARLIAMENTARY REPRESENTATIVES

i)   *Speech in parliament shall be absolutely free and may be reported by the media with absolute freedom.*

ii)   *MPs shall be entitled freely to communicate with their constituents, and vice-versa. An MP's parliamentary office shall not be subject to search or interference, save with the permission of the speaker of the relevant House, who shall if practicable seek the assurance of the attorney-general that the search is necessary for the investigation of a serious crime.*

iii) *Parliament shall not be disturbed, and MPs shall not be subject to arrest or other forcible process in parliament or it precincts, except by the permission of the speaker,*

> *once the attorney-general has confirmed that such*
> *action is necessary to investigate serious crime.*

iv) *In all other respects, MPs shall not be above the law.*

What emerged from the Belinda Neal ('Iguana's Restaurant') affair in 2008 was the strength of feeling among Australians that MPs should not have special privileges ('Don't you know who I am?' is a question they should not ask as a means of throwing their weight around). MPs do have some special privileges they do not need: their VIP passes to sporting events and their 'study tours' to Paris are familiar subjects of ridicule. However, in order to do their democratic duties – to raise constituents' grievances with the government – they do need certain rights. Free speech is a necessity and the 1689 bill of rights guarantees it: MPs cannot be sued for libel over allegations they make in parliament. The speaker has a duty to protect MPs and parliamentary meetings from molestation or pressure, and must turn away policemen, even if they come armed with search warrants, unless there is an emergency or unless the attorney-general confirms that their investigation is into serious crime.

21. RIGHT TO EFFECTIVE JUSTICE

Everyone whose rights and freedoms are violated shall have an effective remedy by way of access to a court or a tribunal empowered to apply the provisions of this charter. The aforesaid court or tribunal shall give a reasoned decision, in language comprehensible to laypersons.

This will not make judges happy, but they should write their judgements for public comprehension and not merely for their own, or their appeal court's, satisfaction. The requirement of an 'effective remedy' by way of access to a court does not require courts to hear every allegation of a violation: they must turn away cases that are frivolous or vexatious, or that do not appear at a short hearing for leave to have any real chance of success.

22. PROHIBITION OF DISCRIMINATION

i)   *Everyone is equal before the law. In all laws made or to be made, every person may be bound alike; and no tenure, estate, charter, degree, birth or place do confer any exemption from the ordinary course of legal proceedings whereunto others are subjected.*

ii) *The enjoyment of the rights and freedoms set forth in this charter shall be secured without discrimination on grounds of age, disability, sex, sexual orientation or gender identity, race, colour, language, religion, political or other opinion, national or social origin, association with a minority, property, birth or other status.*

iii) *In the implementation of government policy, public servants shall in all decisions that involve the rights stated in sections 16–18 above, bear in mind their duty to narrow the gap between rich and poor, and to narrow the gap between Indigenous people and the rest of the community.*

I have been unable to resist incorporation in (i) of the Levellers' great plea in The Agreement of the People for a law that is no respecter of persons. It will serve to remind us that rights have had to be fought for (the English Civil War had, comparatively, more casualties than the First

World War) and that they have engaged English-speaking peoples for much of modern history. Sub-section (iii) is not some Marxist afterthought, it is actually based on a fundamental law suggested by the British government in a White Paper in January 2009. It's worth thinking about.

23. RIGHTS OF CHILDREN
i) *Every child has the right:*
- *a) to a name and a nationality from birth;*
- *b) to family care, parental care, or adequate and appropriate alternative care if removed in accordance with law from a dangerous family environment;*
- *c) to be protected from maltreatment, neglect, abuse or degradation;*
- *d) to be protected from exploitative labour practices;*
- *e) not to be detained except as a matter of last resort and then only for the shortest appropriate period of time.*
ii) *A child's best interests are of special and particular importance in every matter concerning the child.*
iii) *Every person under eighteen years of age who is detained pending or during trial or after conviction must be segregated from detained adults.*

These reflect the most important, enforceable rights in the UN Convention on the Rights of the Child. In (ii), controversially I have made 'the child's best interests' of 'special and particular' but not 'paramount' importance. The interests of their children should not save parents who really deserve imprisonment or deportation.

24. RIGHTS OF DISABLED PEOPLE

The government shall ensure, within its available resources, that all persons who are disabled shall be vouchsafed full enjoyment of the rights set out in this charter without discrimination or diminution on the grounds of their disablement. They shall have the right to live in their community, with choices equal to others, and to participate in their community, and shall in particular have:

   i)   *the opportunity to choose their place of residence and where and with whom they live to the same extent as others;*

   ii) *access to a range of in-house, residential and other community support services, including personal assistance necessary to prevent isolation from the community;*

   iii) *access on an equal basis and in a way that is responsive to their needs, to community services and facilities that are made available to the general population.*

Persons with disabilities are entitled to charter rights without discrimination in any event. This special clause incorporates 'the right to independent living' guaranteed by Article 19 of the UN Convention on the Rights of Persons with Disabilities, ratified by the Australian government in 2008. This is a new right, which has slowly emerged: it began with opposition to the Poor Law, which forcibly removed 'social rejects' from the community. It recently became a policy objective of the European Community and was given a legal dimension by decisions of the European Court of Human Rights. Further impetus was given by The Americans with Disabilities Act (1990), when the Supreme Court interpreted the act as requiring, within state financial resources, rational and fair policies based on the principle that 'unnecessary institutionalisation' should be avoided as far as possible, because:

> Institutional placement of persons who can handle and benefit from community settings perpetuates unwarranted assumptions that persons so isolated are incapable or unworthy of participating in community life . . . confinement in an institution necessarily diminishes the everyday life activities of individuals, including family relations, social contacts, work options, economic independence, educational advancement and cultural enrichment.[3]

The advent of Article 19 of the UN Convention marks the transition of the right to independent living from the realm of policy to that of a fundamental human right. It is not found in these terms – or at all – in older conventions, but all the more reason for Australia to take the lead.

25. RIGHT TO A PRISTINE AND HEALTHY ENVIRONMENT

Everyone has the right:

    i) to an environment that is not harmful to their health or wellbeing;

    ii) to have the environment protected, for the benefit of

present and future generations, through reasonable
legislative and other measures that:

a) prevent pollution and ecological degradation;

b) promote conservation; and protect native flora
and fauna, and areas necessary to maintain
biological diversity and ecosystems;

c) secure ecologically sustainable development
and use of natural resources while promoting
justifiable economic and social development;

d) preserve properties and places of historic or
cultural significance;

e) establish a planning system that ensures
encroachments upon areas of natural beauty or
heritage value are not approved unless by fair,
transparent and non-corrupt process, which takes
that value into account.

iii) to timely and adequate assistance in the event of fire,
flood, cyclone or other natural catastrophe.

There are repeated references in international treaties
and resolutions to the human right to a healthy environment. It has been recognised in the South African constitution and by the Supreme Court of Canada.[4] Australians
proudly sing that 'our land abounds in nature's gifts of
beauty rich and rare', so why not provide nature's gifts
with a measure of legal protection against being given
away to developers?

26. DEROGATION IN TIME OF EMERGENCY

In time of war or other public emergency threatening the life
of the nation the government may take measures derogating

from its obligations under this charter to the extent strictly required by the exigencies of the situation. However, there shall be no derogation from Articles 1, 2(a) and 3.

No emergency can justify slavery, or the death penalty, or torture. It may justify abrogation of other rights, but only to the extent necessary to cope with the particular emergency.

27. SPECIAL RIGHTS OF INDIGENOUS PEOPLE

Indigenous people have distinct cultural rights and must not be denied the right, with other members of their community:

i) *to enjoy their identity and culture;*

ii) *to maintain and use their language;*

iii) *to maintain their kinship ties;*

iv) *to maintain spiritual and material relationships with the land and waters according to their customs of old.*

This right is a work in progress: as Frank Brennan points out, only Aborigines can explain what they want (unity is unlikely) and dialogue across racial boundaries must decide which of their aspirations should be given legal force.[5]

In 1901 the founding fathers of the Commonwealth excluded Aborigines, who were left to the mercy of the states. In 1967 the people voted overwhelmingly to make them part of their own nation, but all that was legally achieved by the referendum was that they were counted in the census and the federal government was given the power to make special laws for them, which would not necessarily be for their benefit. Indigenous rights are given dominance in the preamble and other sections of this charter, which, together with this article, might serve as the basis for a treaty.

My own view is that dignity will only be vouchsafed to our half a million Aborigines if they are given the right to vote for their own parliamentary representatives – two extra senators, perhaps, who might even come to hold the balance of power. (Wouldn't you prefer it to be held by senators such as Noel Pearson, Larissa Behrendt or Marcia Langton, rather than the likes of Brian Harradine or Steve Fielding or the Australian Democrats?)

The advanced nations that have most successfully included their indigenous people – New Zealand and Mauritius, for example – allow them to vote their own representatives into the parliament. It works, but such a constitutional change is outside the scope of this charter or (I suspect) the imagination of our politicians.

28. DUTIES OF AUSTRALIANS

i) *Everyone has duties to the community in which alone the full and free development of their personality is possible.*

ii) *In the exercise of these rights and freedoms, everyone shall be subject to such limitations as are determined by law for the purpose of securing the recognition and respect for the rights and freedoms of others and for meeting the just requirements of public order and general welfare in a democratic society.*

iii) *Nothing in this declaration may be interpreted as implying for any group or person any right to engage in any activity or to perform any act aimed at the destruction of any of the rights or freedoms set forth in this charter.*

iv) *All persons present in Australia (however briefly) have a duty (unless relieved of it by diplomatic or other immunity) to obey the law.*

This important provision makes clear that rights entail responsibility to obey the law, to treat the rights of others with due respect and to support the community. A similar provision is found in the Universal Declaration and most other charters. It is often said by politicians hostile to human rights that such rights are somehow antipathetic to human responsibilities, although in fact they are simply the other side of the same coin. On the fiftieth anniversary of the Universal Declaration, a number of senior politicians, ranging from the impeccably liberal Malcolm Fraser to the impeccably illiberal Lee Kuan Yew, signed up to 'a universal declaration of human responsibilities', which was submitted to the UN.[6]

It turned out to be a fairly colourless list of unenforceable good intentions, such as 'Everyone has a responsibility to promote good and to avoid evil in all things'; 'Every person is infinitely precious and must be protected unconditionally'; 'Every person has a responsibility to speak and act truthfully . . . [but] no one is obliged to tell all the truth to everyone all the time'; 'Sexual partners should accept the responsibility of caring for each others well being'; 'Marriage requires love, loyalty and forgiveness and should aim at guaranteeing security and mutual support'. The UN did not take up the offer to declare these Polonius-like precepts part of international law.

PROCEDURAL PROVISIONS

Some rights – for example, to live in a society free from torture or slavery – should be absolute, while others would be subject to the restrictions that a democratic society must necessarily impose in the public interest, and that a national emergency might reasonably abridge. Charter rights should be capable of assertion only by individuals, except where individuals generally enjoy them through the work of corporations (freedom of speech, for example, requires protection to be extended to newspapers and TV stations). Serious breaches should be compensated by damages, and courts should also be able to grant injunctions to restrain continuing abuses.

All those who exercise governmental or executive power should be subject to the charter, together with private contractors who provide public utilities or services, say by running hospitals, nursing homes or prisons. Parliament should have a standing committee with expert advisors to vet new legislation and draw potential breaches to the notice of MPs, and to receive and consider the need for old legislation to be amended when declarations of incompatibility are made by the courts. Most importantly, there would need to be an education programme for all public-service providers, to promote awareness of their new duties, together with broader community education to inform people of how they can use the charter to improve their lives.

There are other procedural issues involved in the delivery of a bill of rights: precedents abound in the enactments in Britain, New Zealand, and in the ACT and

Victoria. Problems are readily soluble: once the decision to legislate is taken, the technicalities will fall into place.

One thought that may occur to a nervous or uncertain government is to make the charter subject to a 'sunset clause', whereby it operates for, say, five years, providing experience of how it works in practice, and is then re-submitted to parliament, which may amend or repeal it if it turns out – as the critics predict – to undermine democratic government. This way, the proof of the pudding will be in the eating, but the pudding will be capable of regurgitation if it turns out to constipate the system.

In any actual charter, procedural provisions will be drafted at some length and with precision. For example, the draftsman will need to ensure that charter rights have the status of Commonwealth law, which means they will prevail over previous federal legislation, and, by operation of Section 109 of the constitution, will override inconsistent state laws (whether past or future).

I have not attempted what will be a complex drafting exercise: the following provisions are among the most important, and so are sketched here in a broad outline.

i) *Only individual human beings possess the rights granted by this charter. However, the right of freedom of expression may be exercised by media corporations and workplace rights may be exercised by trade unions.*

ii) *It shall be unlawful for a public authority to act in a way that is incompatible with a charter right, unless primary legislation leaves it with no alternative. A public authority includes any court or tribunal and* any person or entity, irrespective of its structure or organisation, whose functions include those of a public nature exercised on behalf of the Commonwealth and/or substantially funded by the Commonwealth. It does not include the Senate or the House of Representatives or any person acting in an official capacity in connection with proceedings in parliament.

iii) This charter shall not be interpreted so as to limit in any way any existing right or freedom under common law or statute.

iv) All statutory provisions must be interpreted, consistently with their purpose, so far as possible in a way that is compatible with the human rights set forth in this charter.

v) The common law must be developed consistently with the human rights set forth in this charter.

vi) Where it is not possible for a court or tribunal to interpret a statute consistently with the charter it shall have the power to grant, as a remedy, a declaration of incompatibility, together with, at its discretion, an order for costs in favour of the party obtaining the said declaration.

vii) The attorney-general shall consider any such declaration and shall report thereon to the parliament.

viii) The attorney-general must, before the second reading of any bill, provide a written compatibility statement in relation to that bill's impact upon the rights granted by this charter. Any provision of the bill that is arguably inconsistent with charter rights must be specifically drawn to the attention of parliament at the second reading of the bill.

ix) A committee to be known as the Joint Standing Committee on Human Rights is to be established as *soon as practicable after the commencement of this act, comprising at least three senators and at least four members of the House of Representatives. The functions of this committee shall include consideration of the attorney-general's compatibility statements and any declaration of incompatibility made by the courts, and to report on these to the relevant minister and to both houses of parliament.*

x) *Any primary legislation passed by this parliament after the charter comes into force may declare that its provisions shall operate notwithstanding any incompatibility, but any such declaration shall have no effect if made in subsidiary legislation or regulations issued by ministers or their departments.*

xi) *The Human Rights and Equal Opportunities Commission is empowered to investigate complaints by individuals or, in relevant cases, by media corporations or trade unions, about alleged violations of this charter, and may deal with them by conciliation or mediation or by a report to parliament or, as a last resort, by bringing or supporting legal action. In this latter event, the Commission shall be accorded standing.*

xii) *Where a court finds that any individual has suffered a serious violation of his or her rights under this charter it may grant a declaration to this effect, and where satisfied that the violation is serious it may make an award of damages up to a maximum amount of $50,000 and may grant injunctive or other relief.*

xiii) (Optional: this is one for the critics.) *This charter shall be re-submitted for debate to both Houses of Parliament*

*as soon as may be practicable five years from its date of
proclamation, and may then be subject to amendment,
re-enactment or repeal as parliament may determine.*

———

Are these rights radical or in any way un-Australian? After
drafting them, I found that the Australian government
promises most of them to those who take up citizenship. In
a leaflet and website, it asks: 'What does being an Australian
mean?' and answers by promising, in return for the pledge
of loyalty, a share in what it terms 'Freedoms, Responsibilities and Privileges'. In the language of legal bargain, it
offers new citizens values and principles 'shared to some
extent by all liberal democracies ... adapted to Australia's
unique setting, moulded and modernised through waves
of settlement by people from all over the world. They
define and symbolise why so many people want to become
Australian'.

What are these defining values? They reflect, often
precisely, the freedoms set out above. Although, curiously,
no mention is made of any right to share in a healthy or
pristine environment, there is no hesitation about promising economic and social rights ('government support
in the form of a social safety net for those who struggle
through life through no fault of their own is part of Australia's egalitarian ethos'). The impression is clearly given to
new (and, for that matter, to old) citizens that they have, by
virtue of their citizenship, a legitimate expectation to these
rights. 'Government agencies and independent courts

must treat everyone fairly', the government proclaims. This is charter language, in the absence of a charter. A bill of rights would make good the government's promise: its enactment should only disquiet those who think that governments should not have to worry about dishonouring the promises they make to their people.

EPILOGUE

On 10 December 2008 – the sixtieth anniversary of the Universal Declaration of Human Rights – the attorney-general announced a national consultation, to be conducted by a four-person committee chaired by Father Frank Brennan, a respected law professor and (on bills of rights) a self-declared fence-sitter.[1] Sitting on the fence (or at least the committee) with him are Tammy Williams, an Aboriginal lawyer, Mick Palmer a former national police commissioner and Mary Kostakidis, a much admired SBS broadcaster. They are tasked to consult on a wide range of views held by the community about human rights and to decide how these rights could be more effectively protected.

The most successful method of promoting human rights was not placed on their agenda, which stated that any option for change 'should . . . not include a constitutionally entrenched bill of rights'.[2] Australia, in so many ways an enthusiastic follower of the United States, was not prepared to consider the method of protecting civil liberties that has helped to make the US great (as President Obama emphasised in his inaugural address), namely via a set of constitutional freedoms ring-fenced from presidents and politicians. It is ironic that a 'national consultation' should from the outset refuse to consider the one system that demonstrably works. This limitation was intended, no doubt, to deter criticism about unelected judges having the power to dictate to elected politicians, although this was the first point that the critics, undeterred, immediately made.

Any hope that goodwill would attend the consultation was soon put in doubt by increasingly strident attacks on lawyers, who would allegedly feast off the charter, and a much publicised distortion of a comment by UK Justice Secretary Jack Straw. On the day the consultation was announced, *The Australian* reported, with a front-page headline, that, 'one of the architects of the British model [Jack Straw] yesterday claimed it had become a "villain's charter".'[3]

This was manna from heaven for charter opponents, none more vehement than the editors of *The Australian*. The next day they gleefully reported: 'The British experience is instructive . . . Jack Straw says he is "greatly frustrated" by how it has been interpreted by the courts, dubbing it the "villain's charter".'[4] A few days later, *The Sydney Morning Herald*'s commentator Gerald Henderson also referred to Jack Straw's description of it as a 'villain's charter'.

Australian newspaper readers would think – they had been made to think – that Jack Straw had dubbed the

Human Rights Act a 'villain's charter'. This was demonstrably untrue. The source of the original story was an interview Straw had given with an anti-Labour British tabloid, *The Daily Mail*, a leading critic of the Human Rights Act. In fact, Straw had defended the act, saying it was 'often blamed unfairly for problems which are in fact caused by other laws . . . people don't tend to notice when the Human Rights Act actually does good in helping to defend individuals from unacceptable abuse'. He went on to say:

> I fully understand that *Mail* readers have concerns about the Human Rights Act. There is a sense that it is a 'villain's charter' . . . I am greatly frustrated by this, not by the concerns, but by some very few judgements that have thrown up these problems.

So he did not describe the act as a 'villain's charter' at all. He said that readers of *The Daily Mail* 'had a sense' of the charter as such – as obviously they would have from the tabloid's critical coverage. And he did not say he was greatly frustrated by how it is being interpreted by the courts: on the contrary he actually said that 'very few' of their judgements had thrown up problems. He was, of course, making the point that as a government minister he was not generally troubled by human rights decisions: a few isolated cases 'greatly frustrated' him, although, as we shall see, what greatly frustrates Mr Straw may greatly please more objective observers. Even if he is right, and there are a few bad decisions, he can always appeal them, and there is no area of law, in Britain or Australia, where there are not a few bad decisions. He meant 'very few' as a compliment to the courts.

To be fair to *The Australian* it has shown a commendable interest in the charter debate and, despite its declared editorial bias, it has published articles in favour of a bill of rights, as well as against.[5] But its editorial distortion of Jack Straw's words was a lapse in journalistic standards.

The Australian press did not, of course, report that British Prime Minister Gordon Brown the very next day praised the Human Rights Act as 'a shield and a safeguard for us all'. Or that the Liberal Democrat leader derided Straw for sucking up to a hostile tabloid: the Liberal Democrats want the act extended to cover economic and social rights.[6] Or that the Conservative leader, David Cameron, at the same time was calling for a home-grown British bill of rights.[7] Or that the Director of Public Prosecutions, Keir Starmer QC, said 'the Human Rights Act is a constitutional instrument of the first importance. It is often overlooked that a lot of the thinking about the rights of victims comes from human rights – under the common law it was much more difficult to argue that victims had a right to an effective investigation'.[8]

And readers were never told what those 'very few' cases were that 'greatly frustrated' Jack Straw in his political position as a government minister. They appear to be those few cases where the courts had stopped him deporting terrorist suspects – persons against whom there was insufficient evidence to put them on trial for any offence – to countries where they would be tortured. It is strongly arguable that

Straw's 'problem' is with morality and the Torture Convention, and not with the courts or the Human Rights Act.

———

Shortly after the consultation in Australia was announced, Judge John Clarke's report on Dr Haneef's case was published. He had been held for fourteen days and charged with serious terrorist offences, despite police having no evidence against him and ASIO saying he was innocent. When granted bail by a magistrate, the minister (Kevin Andrews) cancelled his visa so he would be kept in detention until the 'case' against him collapsed two weeks later. False statements were made to the court to try to keep him in custody. It was an indictment of government ministers, who made 'astonishing' and 'troubling' decisions to deny liberty to an innocent subject persecuted by overzealous federal police. The report pulled some punches, but was no less devastating for that, and it showed how preposterous is the claim that liberty is safe in the hands of politicians.

How did the charterphobes on *The Australian* cope with this revelation? By portentously proclaiming 'there is an existing remedy to protect us from overly enthusiastic politicians and public servants'. And what, pray, is that 'existing remedy'? Why, *The Australian* itself, of course: 'the truth was revealed by this newspaper doing its job … by journalists acting on the public's right to know'.[9]

The claim that journalists can be relied upon to protect the public from human rights abuses by acting on the public's right to know is odd coming from a newspaper that leads a campaign for 'Your Right to Know', which is predicated on the fact that in Australia the public do not have a 'right to know' at all. Media investigations do expose some abuses, and journalism of the class that wins Walkley Awards is not uncommon and deserves salutation. But take it from one who has spent many years defending journalists and newspapers: they cannot possibly expose all abuses, either because they cannot get at the facts, or because sources fear exposure, or editors fear libel actions and damages, or because an individual's ill-treatment is not considered newsworthy. And when they do, often nothing is done about it. Moreover, where journalists do expose scandals, it is usually because of information from confidential sources, very often lawyers or prosecutors or concerned citizens employed by law enforcement agencies (Woodward and Bernstein would never have exposed Watergate without 'Deep Throat' from the FBI). So the idea that the Australian public can sleep easy because its human rights are in the care of journalists is nonsense – nonsense on stilts.

It is, nonetheless, a welcome recognition that they are not entirely safe in the hands of those who are elected, often for their skills in jockeying for party pre-selection rather than for their skills in protecting and promoting human rights. Sometimes the defence of human rights needs the spur of unelected journalists and unelected judges. I do not mean to denigrate politicians – most MPs work hard to take up constituent grievances and genuinely wish to pass laws that respect human rights. Government ministers, too, are, for the most part, dedicated to what they or their party conceives to be the public interest. Public servants usually genuinely wish to serve the public – one pleasing aspect of the British experience (and there are signs that it is being replicated in Victoria) is how awareness of the bill of rights has made them more willing to change wrongful practices, before going to litigation. It will be the task of the national consultation to get out into the suburbs and the satellite towns, to the bush and the remote communities, in order to assess just how often, for all this good faith and goodwill, the legislature, the government and the government's agencies fail to treat fellow Australians with the respect and the civility they deserve.

The consultation will be short: the deadline is 31 July 2009. My great concern is that members of the public will not come forward with concrete reasons for a bill because they think them too minor. They may think that human rights violations only concern loss of liberty or physical pain or deportation, the kind of ordeal suffered by Haneef and Hicks and Rau. But, as I have tried to explain in this book, a charter is for everyone – it is based on our fundamental right to have our dignity respected by officialdom.

I am going to tell the commission about the way old people are treated in the charter-phobic state of New South Wales. I will give an example of the proud ex-naval officer, who wore his ex-naval beard with pride until he was admitted to a state hospital, where for no reason relevant to his treatment it was forcibly shaved off. I am going to tell of the old wartime pilot, who had driven a car for seventy years and was (quite rightly) obliged by law to take a test. When he failed it, you know what they did – what they do to all old people who fail driving tests in New South Wales? They grabbed from his hands the licence he had held for seventy years and then, to humiliate him, they cut it up in front of his eyes. So much for the respect for human dignity after all those years of government by Bob Carr! A stupid, pointless and unthinking humiliation, never noticed by parliament, but typical, I'm sure, of other more seriously stupid, pointless and unthinkingly cruel practices that can develop in the public service unless public servants are made to remember that the people they deal with deserve a little dignity.

So don't hold back, don't feel restrained from talking about liberty – its history and its principles and the moral and emotional satisfaction of living in a nation that upholds it. Your very appearance gives the lie to the whinging comms, who claim that charters are conspiracies by the elite to deprive the people of the power of their government and elected representatives. The truth is that charters return some of that power to the people, by allowing them to challenge decisions that lack fairness or scruple or consistency, made by those George Orwell described as 'the striped-trousered ones who rule' (although 'striped trousers' in Canberra is a state of mind, not a form of dress). Civil liberties are not privileges granted at the discretion of the powerful, they are rights capable of assertion by members of the public. That's why a charter is a statute of liberty, because it takes a small amount of power back from the government and the MPs and the public service, and restores it to the people who, in any democracy, are entitled to it, and, in any advanced democracy other than Australia, actually possess it.

Notes

Chapter 1: Over the Sea from Skye

1. *Who Do You Think You Are?* was produced by Artemis Films and Film Australia, SBS Television. This episode was shown on 27 January 2008.

2. Legal definition of 'race' has moved beyond biological or eugenic phenotypes to cover a people whose characteristics come from their shared history, institutions and communal identity. *The Shorter Oxford English Dictionary* defines a race simply as 'a group of persons ... connected by common descent or origin'. Australian Chief Justice Robert French points out that the fact of membership of a race is a cultural, not a biological, construct. See H. P. Lee and George Winterton, *Australian Constitutional Landmarks*, Cambridge University Press, 2003, chapter 8, 'The Race Power: A Constitutional Chimera'.

3. See, for example, Ian F. Haney-Lopez, 'The Social Construction of Race' in Julie Rivkin and Michael Ryan (eds), *Literary Theory: An Anthology*, Blackwell Publishing,

2004; Richard Delgado and Jean Stefancic (eds), *Critical Race Theory: The Cutting Edge*, Temple University Press, 2000; and Michael Omi and Henry Winant, *Racial Formation in the United States*, Routledge, 1994.

4. 'For those who've come across the seas / We've boundless plains to share', asserts the second verse of 'Advance Australia Fair', proclaimed in 1984 as the national anthem. The government should consider reversing the decision to impose this awful dirge on our children at school assemblies and on our medal-winning Olympians. The astonishing, beautiful and different 'Waltzing Matilda', with its haunting story of a homeless man who evades the police and commits suicide, would make the world's most interesting (and most tuneful) anthem.

5. The very first overseas connections with Australia were by Macassan traders from Sulawesi fishing for trepang (sea cucumbers) prized by the Chinese for their apparent aphrodisiac qualities. The traders formed some close attachments with the Yolngu people of Arnhem Land over a century before the First Fleet.

6. See www.citizenship.com.au: *Becoming an Australian Citizen, Part 1: what does it mean to be an Australian?*

7. Geoffrey Robertson QC, *Freedom, the Individual and the Law*, Penguin Books, 1993.

8. *The Australian*: 31 October 2007; 29 February 2008; 9 February 2008; 7 February 2008; 11 April 2008; 2 April 2008.

9. Andrew Byrnes, Hilary Charlesworth, Gabrielle McKinnon, *Bills of Rights in Australia*, UNSW Press, 2009, chapters 4 and 5.

10. See, for example, *Pratt and Morgan* (1994) 2 AC 1 (death penalty); *Bradshaw v. Attorney-General* (1995) 1 WLR 936 (death penalty); *Nguyen Tuan Cuong v. Director of Immigration* (1996) 7 HK PLR 19 (refugees – Privy Council); *Republic of Fiji v. Prasad* (2001) NZAR 385 (democracy); *Lennox Phillip v. DPP* (1992) 1 AC 545 (habeas corpus).

Chapter 2: The Rights of Humankind

1. I tell of the civil liberties struggles that led to the English Civil War in *The Tyrannicide Brief*, Vintage, 2006, chapters 1–3.
2. Geoffrey Robertson, *The Levellers: the Putney Debates*, Verso, 2007, p. 69.
3. Ibid, p. 54.
4. Robertson, *The Tyrannicide Brief*, p. 62.
5. *Bushell's Case* (1670) State Trials 999.
6. *Entick v. Carrington*, 19 State J, 1029–66.
7. Geoffrey Robertson, *Crimes Against Humanity*, Penguin 2006, p. 12.
8. *Marbury v. Madison* (1803) 5 US (1 Cranch) 137 at 163.
9. Jeremy Bentham, *Supply without burthen or escheat Vice Taxation*, 1794, objection V; James Spigelman (ed. Tim Castle), *Speeches of a Chief Justice*, CS2N Publishing, 2008, p. 312.
10. Robertson, *Crimes Against Humanity*, pp. 26 ff.
11. For the story of the Australian delegation and Evatt's influence on the Universal Declaration drafting, see Annemarie Devereux, *Australia and the Birth*

of the International Bill of Rights 1946–1966, The Federation Press, 2005. All quotations from the Australian delegation in this section of the book are taken from this article. The wider story of the drafting of the declaration is found in Johannes Morsink, *The Universal Declaration of Human Rights,* University of Pennsylvania Press, 1999.

12. Immanuel Kant (tr. L. W. Beck), *Foundations of the Metaphysics of Morals,* Prentice Hall, 1990, pp. 49–50.

13. Kenneth Roth and Minky Worden (eds), *Torture,* The New Press, 2005, foreword; Richard Ashby Wilson (ed.), 'Fair Trials for Terrorists', *Human Rights and the War on Terror,* Cambridge University Press, 2005.

14. Ronald Dworkin, *A Bill of Rights for Britain,* Chatto & Windus, 1990, p. 13, citing French historian François Furet.

15. It is said that John Howard chose Dyson Haydon to be a High Court judge after reading his attack on High Court 'activists' in the right-wing magazine *Quadrant,* and that Kevin Rudd chose a Western Australian, Robert French, as chief justice over James Spigelman because Victorian members of his cabinet objected to having another chief justice from New South Wales. These particular choices were fine, but what a strange way to make them!

Chapter 3: So-called 'Rights' of Australians

1. The Australian constitution, Sections 1, 59, 60, 61 and 68.

www.aph.gov.au/Senate/general/constitution/index.htm

2. *R v. Wilson; ex parte Kisch* (1934) 52 CLR 234.

3. *Spratt v. Hermes* (1965) 114 CLR 226 at 244.

4. *Roach v. Electoral Commissioner* (2007) HCA 43.

5. *Krygger v. Williams* (1912) 15 CLR 366. A seventeen-year-old claimed that military training was against his conscience and the will of God, and hence his conscription contravened Section 116, which guarantees 'the free exercise of any religion'. The High Court interpreted this right narrowly, to mean liberty to engage in church rites and worship rather than to observe its teachings (however dogmatic), about the good and godly life. During the Vietnam conscription era, the court at least allowed conscientious objection if it was to be 'deep-seated and compelling' – *R v. District Court, ex parte White*, 116 CLR 644 – but the restrictive definition of Section 116 still stands.

6. Report from the Select Committee on Aborigines (British settlements), House of Commons, 26 June 1837, p. 14, where the committee adopted a statement by Sir Gilbert Murray: 'the adoption of any line of conduct, having for its avowed or secret object the extinction of the native race, could not fail to leave an indelible stain upon the British government'.

7. Lee and Winterton, *Australian Constitutional Landmarks*, p. 185.

8. See the discussion in the *Hindmarsh Bridge Case* – *Kartinyeri v. Commonwealth* (1998) 195 CLR 337, where only Justice Kirby was of the opinion that the federal parliament could not legislate to disadvantage, or discriminate against, Aborigines.

9. *Kruger v. Commonwealth* (1997) 190 CLR 1.

10. Brian Burdekin, 'Common law fails to protect disadvantaged people', *Sydney Morning Herald*, 15 December 2008.

11. 'A Charter of Rights for Tasmania', Tasmanian Law Reform Institute, 16 October 2007, chapter 2.2.

12. Australia, in John Howard's phrase, a 'model member of the UN', has ratified the protocols that enable its record to be scrutinised by the Human Rights Committee, the Committee Against Torture and the Committee on the Elimination of Racial Discrimination. But when the latter committee, in 2000, took issue with the nation's treatment of Aborigines, the government petulantly responded with the claim that UN criticism of its record was 'unacceptable'.

Chapter 4: Advance of Fair Australia

1. As Blackstone put it in his enormously influential *Commentaries on the Laws of England* (commentary I, 16) published in 1758: 'If an uninhabited colony is discovered and planted by English subjects, all the English laws are immediately there in force. For as the law is the birthright of every subject, so wherever they go they carry their laws with them'. This rule was subject only to the proviso that conditions in the colony had to permit their application.

2. Peter Cochrane, *Australian Greats*, Random House Australia, 2008, p. 65.

3. Robertson, *The Levellers*, p. 54.

4. Manning Clark, *A History of Australia*, Penguin Books, 1986, pp. 108–9.

5. A *Voyage to Terra Australis*. Flinders received the book proofs for his work in London a few hours before his death from a venereal disease picked up during the seven years he spent as a prisoner of the French in Mauritius. Governor Macquarie used the name in his official dispatches and recommended that it be adopted for the continent: in 1824 the British Admiralty agreed.

6. Michael Frayn, *Copenhagen*, Methuen, 1998.

7. Margaret Steven, *First Impressions: British Discovery of Australia*, British Museum, 1988, p. 89.

8. David Neal, *The Rule of Law in a Penal Colony: Law and Power in Early New South Wales*, Cambridge University Press, 1991, chapter 7, 'The Campaign for Trial by Jury'.

9. Henry Lawson, 'Freedom on the Wallaby', *Selected Poems of Henry Lawson*, Angus & Robertson, 1918.

10. Geoffrey Robertson, 'As Brave as Tom Curnow', Peter Cochrane, *Australian Greats*, pp. 191–3.

11. Geoffrey Robertson and Andrew Nicol, *Robertson and Nicol on Media Law*, Sweet & Maxwell 2007 and Penguin 2008, chapter 1, 'Freedom of Expression'.

12. Spigelman, *Speeches of a Chief Justice*, 'Foundations of the Freedom of the Press in Australia', p. 379.

13. A Menzies-era cabinet minister told me, many years ago, that he and his colleagues were all in favour of *Lady Chatterley*'s admission to Australia until Sir Robert strode into the room and told them it was a book he would never allow his wife, Dame Pattie, to read.

14. *Lange v. Australian Broadcasting Corporation* (1997) 187 CLR 520. The 'implication' extends only to 'political or governmental matters' that are relevent to voters.

15. *Harvey v. County Court Victoria* (2006) VSW 293. The journalists were convicted of contempt of court and fined $7000 each, for obeying their conscience and their professional code of conduct.

16. Allan Kessing, a former Australian customs officer, was convicted in 2007 and given a nine-month suspended prison sentence for telling the media about security problems at airports that customs had for years failed to remedy. Only when the media reported this did the government act: it spent $200 million dollars to remedy the defects and a further million to prosecute Kessing. Treasurer Connolly was able to cover up the Treasury's failures to protect first homebuyers from fraud: see *McKinnon v. Secretary, Department of Treasury* (2006) 229 ALR 187.

17. *Coleman v. Australia* 1157/2003; for the High Court decision see *Coleman v. Power* (2004) 201 CLR 1.

Chapter 5: The Case for a Statutory Charter

1. Hillaire Belloc, 'Jim', *Selected Cautionary Verses*, Penguin Books, 1958.

2. 'A WA Human Rights Act', report of the Consultation Committee for a proposed WA Human Rights Act, November 2007.

3. Byrnes *et al.*, *Bills of Rights in Australia*, chapter 4.

4. See *General Television*, 2008, BSCA 49. Australian (and

especially Victorian) judges have been unreceptive to free-speech rights, especially when they think juries might be influenced by media comment. But jurors should not be treated as simpletons and, unless a fair trial is endangered because a defendant is subject to media vilification, the powers of trial judges to cure prejudice by jury directions should be sufficient to obviate any need to impose suppression orders or prosecute editors for contempt.

5. 'First Steps Forward: the 2007 report on the operation of the charter of human rights and responsibilities', Victorian Equal Opportunities and Human Rights Commission, 2008, p. 42; Byrnes et al., Bills of Rights in Australia, chapter 5.

6. Information provided to the author by Philip Lynch, Director of the Human Rights Law Resource Centre.

7. The case was *Parker v. The Queen* (1963) 111 CLR 610, when the patience of the loyal anglophiles in the Australian High Court towards the less able British law lords sitting above them on the Privy Council finally snapped. The law lords lacked any real understanding of criminal law, and had recently delivered a decision that had wrongly widened the law of murder. 'They are hanging men for manslaughter in England now,' said one shocked Australian judge. So, in *Parker's Case*, Chief Justice Dixon at last declared that the Australian High Court would no longer be bound to follow British court decisions, although they would remain influential.

8. *A v. Secretary of State for the Home Office* (2004) UK HL 56; *Al-Kateb v. Godwin* (2004) 219 CLR 562.

9. *Peck v. United Kingdom* (2003) 36 EHRR 41.

10. Kenneth Karst, 'Paths to belonging: the constitution and cultural identity', 64 *North Carolina Law Review*, 303 (1968) especially at 361–77; Donald J. Devine, *The Political Culture of the United States*, Little, Brown and Co, 1972, pp. 116–19 and 141–3.

11. Charles Taylor, 'Can Canada Survive the Charter?', 15 *Alberta Law Review*, 1992, pp. 427–31; Peter Russell *et al*, *The Clash of Rights*, Yale University Press, 1996, pp. 157–72.

12. 'A WA Human Rights Act', p. 69.

13. Varun Gauri and Daniel Brinks, 'The impact of legal strategies for claiming economic and social rights', *ESR Review*, vol. 8, no 2.

14. A Harvard School of Public Health study, published in the *Journal of Acquired Immune Deficiency Syndromes* in November 2008, concludes that 35,000 babies were born with HIV-AIDS as a consequence of the Mbeki government decision not to distribute anti-retroviral drugs. Mbeki seemed to think that HIV-AIDS was a Western plot, while his health minister, Manto Tshabalala-Msimang ('Dr Beetroot'), said it could be cured by mixing wild garlic with African potato. The Harvard study estimated that in total 330,000 had died because of the government's inaction, before the constitutional court ordered it to act rationally and to make the drugs available.

15. *Minister of Health v. Treatment Action Campaign* (2002) 5 SA 721.

16. *Government of South Africa v. Grootbloom* (2001) 1 SA 46.

17. Global Gender Gap report, World Economic Forum,

November 2008.

18. 'Child Poverty' report on UNICEF economy statistics, 24 November 2008.

19. *New York Times Co v. Sullivan* 401 US 265.

20. *Goodwin v. UK* (1996) 22 EHRR 123, para 39.

21. US law offers no protection to American journalists if they refuse to answer grand jury questions: *Branzburg v. Hayes* (1972) 408 US 665.

22. 'No magic bullet exists to protect free speech', *The Australian*, 31 August 2007.

23. *Reynolds v. Times Newspapers* (2001) 2 AC 127.

24. *Jameel v. Wall Street Journal* (Europe) (2006) 3 WLR 642.

25. *S (A Child) identification: restriction on publication* (2005) 1 AC 593.

Chapter 6: The British Experience

1. Bentham, *Supply without Burthen*, objection V.

2. H. G. Wells, *The New World Order*, Penguin Books, 1939.

3. *Sunday Times v. UK* (1979) 2 EHRR 245.

4. Robertson, *Freedom, the individual and the law*, p. 511.

5. *Golder v. UK ECHR* series A, vol 18 (1975).

6. *Tim Hector v. Attorney-General of Antigua* (1990) 2 AC 312.

7. The Court of Final Appeal is really a court of penultimate appeal, since the Chinese communist party can veto any of its decisions. However, it has only done so on one occasion, ordering Sir Anthony to eat his words on the right of refugee families to settle in the province.

See *Ng Sin Tang and others v. Director of Immigration* (2002) HKCV 13 (10 January 2002).

8. Human Rights Act, 1998, Section 19.

9. Paul Kelly, 'Uncharted waters', *The Australian*, 13 December 2008.

10. *Blood and Tarbuck v. Secretary of State for Health*, High Court (Sullivan J) (28 February 2003). Amended by the Human Fertilisation (Deceased Fathers) Act 2003.

11. *Bellinger v. Bellinger* (2003) UK HL 21. Remedied by the Gender Recognition Act 2004.

12. *R (on the application of M) v. Secretary of State for Health* (2003) EWHC 1094: to be amended in the next Mental Health Bill.

13. Amended by the Sexual Offences Act (2003) s.139, 140, Schedule 6 (para 4) and Schedule 7.

14. *R (on the application of H) v. Mental Health Review Tribunal* (2001) EWCA Civ 417. Amended by the National Immigration and Asylum Act 2002, s. 125.

15. *International Transport Roth GmbH v. Secretary of State for the Home Department* (2002) EWCA Civ 178.

16. *R v. Secretary of State for the Home Department ex parte D* (2002) EWHC 2805. Amended by the Criminal Justice Act 2003, s. 295.

17. *R (on the application of Hooper) v. Secretary of State for Work and Pensions* (2003) EWCA Civ 875. Amendment already in force by the time of the decision.

18. *R v. Westminster City Council and Secretary of State* (2004) EWHC 2191; EWCA Civ 1184, amended in Housing and Regeneration Act, 2008.

19. *Smith v. Scott* (2007) CSIH 9 (registration appeal court for Scotland); Jack Straw's announcement of public consultation: *Hansard*, 10 September 2008, column 1982w.

20. *R (Clift et al) v. Secretary of State for the Home Department* (2006) UK HL 54. This was remedied in the Criminal Justice and Immigration Act 2008.

21. *A and others v. Secretary of State for the Home Department* (2004) UK HL 56. The offending provisions were repealed by the Prevention of Terrorism Act 2005, which put in place a new regime of control orders.

22. Lord Hoffman in *R v. Secretary of State for the Home Department, ex parte Simms* (2000) 2 AC 115 at 131.

23. *Ghaidan v. Godin-Mendoza* (2004) UK HL 30.

24. House of Lords and House of Commons, Joint Committee on Human Rights, 'The Human Rights Act: the DCA and Home Office Reviews', 2005–6, 32nd report, November 2006.

25. *Lee v. Leeds CC* (2002) 1WLR 1488.

26. *A and B v. East Sussex CC* (2003) EWCA Civ 1170.

27. House of Lords and House of Commons, Joint Committee on Human Rights, 'The Human Rights Act', para 74.

28. *The Human Rights Act: Changing Lives*, British Institute of Human Rights, second edition, press release, 24 November 2008.

29. *Beaulane Properties v. Palmer* (2005) EWHC 1071.

30. *Andrews v. The Reading Borough Council* (2005) EWHC 256.

31. *Amin v. Secretary of State for the Home Department* (2004) 1 AC 653.

32. *A v. Secretary of State for the Home Department* (2005) 2 AC 68, para 18.

33. Geoffrey Robertson, *People Against the Press*, Quartet Books, 1983; *Robertson and Nicol on Media Law*, chapter 14; 'Report of the Committee for Privacy HMSO', 1990, p. 1102; Sir David Calcutt, 'Review of Press Self-Regulation', 1993, cm 2135.

34. *Campbell v. MGN Limited* (2004) UKHL 22.

35. *Moseley v. Group Newspapers Ltd* (2008) EWHC 1777.

36. *Robertson v. Wakefield District Council* (2002) QB 1052.

37. For Straw's actual comment and Cameron's plans for a new British bill of rights see 'Jack Straw reveals: why I want to change the law', *The Daily Mail*, 8 December 2008. Gordon Brown's comments were made at an event to mark the sixtieth anniversary of the Universal Declaration.

38. Nick Clegg, 'Freedom is taking a battering under knee-jerk New Labour' *The Guardian*, 10 December 2008.

Chapter 7: Critics

1. George Pell, 'Four Freedoms: the Argument against a Charter of Rights', an address to the Brisbane Institute, 29 April 2008. Pell himself went on to say (in a sentence that critics who use his example never quote), 'A courageous judge or court could undoubtedly make a difference by faithfully administering the law, but Mugabe's government has largely taken care of that danger.'

2. Robertson, *Crimes Against Humanity*, pp. 18 and 23–6.
3. *Connolly v. DPP* (2007) EWHC 237, ADM.
4. *Bowman v. UK* (1998) 26 EHRR 1.
5. *The Australian*, 24 April 2008.
6. *The Australian*, 11 December 2008; Janet Albrechtsen, 'Keep power with the people', *The Australian*, 10 December 2008.
7. The Mercer Report, 'Renumeration Recommendations', October 2006, found that salaries for lawyers in community law centres were only 60–70 per cent of the salaries of lawyers with comparable experience in the public service. The award for cadet journalists gives them salaries comparable to more experienced community centre lawyers – ranging from $43,000 for cadets fresh from school to $57,000 for a 'Grade 3' journalist who has 'completed the basic educational and training requirements' and has had sufficient practical experience 'to carry out a range of routine assignments competently under direction'.
8. The example that emphatically refutes the 'fat cat' caricature is the *Vickie Roach Case*, the most important civil liberties challenge in recent years, when the High Court found an 'implied right' to vote in the constitution and struck down a 2006 law that disenfranchised all prisoners. The case was handled by the Human Rights Resource Centre lawyers (average salary $50,000) and was run entirely on a *pro bono* basis, with all barristers and the large law firm Allens Arthur Robinson donating its services free of charge. Their efforts achieved a significant (albeit limited) democratic right for Australians: the right not to be

unreasonably disenfranchised by the government. When cases actually reach court the government defending them will also instruct lawyers, of course, but solicitors in the public service are on modest salaries and presumably they will use government counsel – the solicitor-general – rather than hire top price QCs from the private bar.

9. 'Carr warns on a bill of rights push', *The Australian*, 26 April 2007.

10. Glenn Milne, 'Liberals aim to wedge Labor on bill of rights', *The Australian*, 11 August 2008.

11. Renee Viellaris, 'Bill of rights to create Star Chamber', *The Courier-Mail*, 15 August 2008.

12. Bob Carr, submission to Standing Committee on Law and Justice inquiry, 2002.

13. Bob Carr, 'Lawyers are already drunk with power', *The Australian*, 24 April 2008. My thanks to Kate McGarrity of the Gilbert and Tobin Law Centre at the University of New South Wales, who has written a paper comprehensively refuting the claims Bob Carr makes in his article.

14. *R v. Home Secretary, ex parte Wayne Thomas Black*, Court of Appeal (15 April 2008); *R (on the application of Black) v. Secretary of State for Justice* (2009) UK HL1 (21 January 2001), especially Lord Roger at para 50.

15. *A v. Home Office*, decision of Mitting J (11 April 2008). An appeal decision is awaited.

16. For those interested in the truth of the 'slop-out' saga, see *Napier v. Scottish Ministers* (2001), Court of Session, 26 June, where the court pointed out that the government had known for years that the 'slopping-out'

arrangements were gross and inadequate, and in likely breach of Article 3. The second case, *Napier v. Scottish Ministers No. 2* (2005) SC 229 confirmed that the 'slop-out' regime was in breach: the damages, however, were granted for negligence.

17. Janet Albrechtsen, 'Even young progressives don't want to give unelected judges more power', *The Australian*, 7 June 2008.
18. Channel 9, *60 Minutes*, 22 April 2007.
19. 'A bill to dodge', *The Australian*, 3 October 2008.
20. Janet Albrechtsen, 'Death to democracy', *The Australian*, 26 June 2002.
21. Janet Albrechtsen, 'Beware, charted waters can have murky depths', *The Australian*, 18 April 2007.
22. Janet Albrechtsen, *The Australian*: 18 April 2008; 23 April 2008; 18 April 2008.
23. James Allen, 'Political correctness stifles debate, *The Australian*, 3 October 2007.
24. James Allen, *The Australian*: 14 December 2007, 29 February 2008, 2 April 2008, 11 April 2008, 3 October 2008, 11 August 2008, 27 April 2007, 19 October 2007, 14 December 2007.
25. James Allen, 'Don't give judges any more power', *The Australian*, 7 February 2008.
26. James Allen, *The Australian*, 27 April 2007; 29 February 2008.
27. James Allen, *The Australian*, 11 April 2008; 2 April 2008.
28. *R* (on the application of Bernard) *v. Enfield*, NBLBC (2002) EWHC 2282 (admin) at para 39 per Sullivan J.

Chapter 8: The Statute of Liberty

1. At least he did so in episode two of the mini-series *John Adams*, which Americans treat as historical truth.

2. *Chorzow Factory Case* (1928) PCIJ series A, no. 17.

3. *Olmstead v. LC*, 527 US 581 (1999); L. Clements and C. Parker, 'The UN Convention on the Rights of Persons with Disabilities: a new right to independent living', *European Human Rights Law Review*, issue 4, 2008, pp. 508–23.

4. *R v. Canadian Pacific Ltd* (1995) 125 DLR (4th) 385 which, at 417–18, approved the Law Commission statement in 'Crimes Against the Environment' (working paper 44, The Commission, Ottawa, 1985), which concluded on p. 8 that 'a fundamental and widely shared value is indeed seriously contravened by some environmental pollution, a value which we will refer to as *the right to a safe environment*' [my italics]. The Supreme Court approved the same passage again in the subsequent case of *R v. Hydro Quebec* (1997) 3 SCR 213 at para 124.

5. Frank Brennan, *Legislating Liberty: a bill of rights for Australia?*, University of Queensland Press, 1998.

6. The InterAction Council, 'A Universal Declaration of Human Responsibilities,' 1 September 1997.

Epilogue

1. Some critics have doubted the openness of Frank Brennan's mind, having misread (or not read) his 1998 book entitled *Legislating Liberty: a bill of rights for Australia?* This work certainly exposed the failure

of the common law in Australia, but its solution was a 'Commonwealth Charter of Espoused Rights', which applied only to 'proposed laws', and merely gave citizens the opportunity to petition a Senate committee to ask the senators to ask the politicians to institute an inquiry. Citizens can always petition parliament – it is an ancient, right and this 'Clayton's Charter' was really no charter at all (as the author concedes, it is simply a means of 'reconstituting Australia without a bill of rights'). Father Brennan wrote his book before the Human Rights Act in Britain, which is now the exemplar: his ultra-minimalist model of 1998 may not be his preference in 2009.

2. Frank Brennan, 'Debate terms not slanted towards a bill', *The Australian*, 22 December 2008.

3. *The Australian*, 10 December 2008; editorial, *The Australian*, 11 December 2008

4. 'Balance of power worth defending', *The Australian*, 11 December 2008.

5. For example, Mike Steketee, 'Judges have their place', *Weekend Australian*, 27–28 December 2008. This article is an excellent example of balanced reporting by the paper's national affairs editor, and at last put the quotation from Jack Straw in its proper perspective.

6. Nick Clegg, 'Freedom is taking a battering under kneejerk New Labour', *The Guardian*, 10 December 2008.

7. Benedict Brogan and Paul Waugh, 'Cameron "will scrap Human Rights Act" in campaign for UK Bill of Rights', *The Daily Mail*, 8 December 2008.

8. Afua Hirsch, 'Superdatabase tracking all calls and emails legitimate, says DPP', *The Guardian*, 9 January 2009.

9. 'Scrutiny can prevent another Haneef case', *The Australian*, 24 December 2008.

ACKNOWLEDGEMENTS

I have written this book in a London autumn, where distance may have lent enchantment to my view of Australia, although I have revised it during a Christmas in Sydney, where the view is more enchanting than ever. Thanks to Margie Seale, Nikki Christer and Karen Reid at Random House. I could not have delivered without Penny Cross's ability to make sense of my manuscript, and I am enormously grateful to Catherine Hill for her editorship. For research my thanks to Jen Robinson at Oxford and Alex Gask at Doughty Street Chambers, while Phil Lynch at the Victorian Centre for Human Rights, Ed Santow and Kate McGarrity at the Gilbert and Tobin Centre UNSW, Justice Kate O'Regan of the South African Constitutional Court, Tim Robertson SC, Kathy Lette and Maureen Carozza have been helpful in various ways. And John Mortimer, thanks for the memories: your dedication to liberty will still be an inspiration.